GLORY CHASERS

Discovering God's Glory in Unexpected Places

DORINA LAZO GILMORE

Copyright © 2017 Dorina Lazo Gilmore

First printing 2017, Second printing 2018

No part of this book may be reproduced or transmitted in any form or by any means electronic or mechanical, including photocopying and recording, or by any information storage or retrieval system, except as may be expressly permitted in writing by the author. Requests should be addressed in writing through www.DorinaGilmore.com.

ISBN-13: 978-1975712525
ISBN-10: 1975712528

Book cover and interior designer: Tara Mayberry, TeaBerry Creative
Author photo: Allison Vasquez

Scripture quotations marked (ESV) are from the ESV® Bible (The Holy Bible, English Standard Version®), copyright © 2001 by Crossway, a publishing ministry of Good News Publishers. Used by permission. All rights reserved.

Scripture quotations marked (HCSB) are taken from the Holman Christian Standard Bible®, Copyright © 1999, 2000, 2002, 2003, 2009 by Holman Bible Publishers. Used by permission. Holman Christian Standard Bible®, Holman CSB®, and HCSB® are federally registered trademarks of Holman Bible Publishers.

Scripture quotations marked (NIV) are taken from the THE HOLY BIBLE, NEW INTERNATIONAL VERSION®, NIV® Copyright © 1973, 1978, 1984, 2011 by Biblica, Inc.® Used by permission. All rights reserved worldwide.

Scripture quotations marked (NLT) are taken from the Holy Bible, New Living Translation, copyright © 1996, 2004, 2007 by Tyndale House Foundation. Used by permission of Tyndale House Publishers, Inc., Carol Stream, Illinois 60188. All rights reserved.

Scripture quotations marked (MSG) are taken from The Message. Copyright © 1993, 1994, 1995, 1996, 2000, 2001, 2002. Used by permission of NavPress Publishing Group.

To order additional copies of this resource, order online through www.dorinagilmore.com.

DORINA LAZO GILMORE is a published writer, blogger, and teacher. She has published three books for children, including the award-winning *Cora Cooks Pancit*. She has also published a volume of poetry and several chapters in collaborative books. Dorina shares her words around the interwebs at places such as For Every Mom, Kindred Mom, In All Things, and on her personal blog at www.DorinaGilmore.com. She is passionate about sharing the hope we have in Jesus Christ with women of all ages and cultures.

Dorina is married and a mama to three active girls. When she isn't taxi driving her girls to school and activities, Dorina loves to run marathons, visit the ocean, curl up with a book, or gather people around her table for a good meal.

Learn more about Dorina's work and join her Glorygram list at www.DorinaGilmore.com. Use the hashtag #GloryChasers on social media.

*For my little Glory Chasers,
Meilani, Giada and Zayla,
who run with such courage
and bolster their mama's faith.*

CONTENTS

ONE	Invitation to the Table 1
TWO	Creation 9
THREE	Presence 25
FOUR	Worship 43
FIVE	Fame 57
SIX	Suffering 75
SEVEN	Community 91
EIGHT	Justice 109
NINE	Heaven 129
TEN	Closing Thoughts: Beauty From Ashes 147

Leader Guide 156

End Notes 167

Acknowledgements 171

WEEK ONE
INVITATION TO THE TABLE

For the last several years, a small group of my friends have gathered just after the turn of the New Year for what we affectionately call a Word party. Every year the party looks a little different. We let the kids (12 among the 5 of us now) run wild in the yard, jump on the trampoline, or play sardines in the bedrooms while the mamas gather around the table. My friend Amy is a tea connoisseur, so she's particular about getting the chai brewed just right with a dash of milk, and it's heavenly. Carla is sure to be in the kitchen cooking up something like a frittata with garden-fresh vegetables. Yasmin typically brings something with brie because brie makes everything better. Terry and I are usually given special assignments. She's the queen of homemade mango salsa accompanied by those delectable tortilla chips from the corner store. The mamas text me early to make sure I'll bring my famous Chicken Salad Wonton Cups—a recipe I created years ago for a contest at the Big Fresno Fair. One year our Word party even incorporated an art project. Terry brought old wood pallets. Amy brought her treasure box of paints, brushes and stencils so we could all create a piece for our home with our theme word on it.

Beyond the excuse for delectable food and heavenly chai, our Word parties are a chance to reflect on the past year and to look into the future with eager eyes. We each choose one word to embody our year. We commit to studying, following, contemplating, cradling, dwelling on that word for the entire 365 days. Until we meet again. Some of us journal our discoveries.

> **Bonus Glory:**
> *Jesus said to her, "Did I not tell you that if you believed you would see the GLORY of GOD?"*

Others peck out late-night text messages to the group with Bible verses or quotes or "word sightings" in our daily lives. At the party, we each have the assignment of tracing what God has taught us about that word in the past year. With great anticipation, we also reveal our word for the coming year and pray over them together.

This gathering has become sacred through the years. Sacred, not quiet and perfect like stepping into an ornate church somewhere in Europe flanked with breathtaking stain-glassed windows, but sacred generally including a noisily nursing baby, the sounds of video games piping through the living room and a dog barking at the side door. This time is sacred. It is a chance to share our faith stories in community, an opportunity to offer up tearful reflections and spur each other on to greater faith.

At the close of 2013, I started thinking about my word. I started thinking, praying, pondering. When the word *glory* wormed its way into my heart, I was surprised. *Glory?* It didn't seem to flow with the words from years past. I had already chosen thanksgiving, then joy, and one year I had settled on two words: grace and mercy because I couldn't choose just one. My friends were choosing words like worship and community. How did glory fit there? At first blush, glory conjured up images of war heroes and athletes defying great odds to gain victory. Glory seemed complex—even self-serving, loud, and boisterous. Somehow it didn't speak of the quiet meditation I'd experienced before.

I tried to dismiss it. Maybe I could choose a nicer word. Something like Love? Peace? Simplicity? Rest? Words I could feel good about plastering on my wall and exploring with my heart. Somehow that crazy glory word just kept coming back to me. Every song, every billboard, every sermon, every movie, every commercial, every Bible verse seemed to incorporate that word somehow. I was intrigued. I needed to know more. What did it mean? Why was glory important to the gospel? How was it pertinent to me?

Little did I know that this single, 5-letter word would be the thing God would use to transform me, inspire me, lift me, and carry me through the most difficult year of my entire life. This would be the beginning of tracing His glory story in the most unexpected places, in the most surprising ways.

I'm inviting you to join me on a journey of discovery. This whole thing is a wild experiment, a treasure hunt, a quest, an expedition, a challenge, an avenue for all of us to join hearts in search of God's glory. I am positioning myself as a Sherpa—a guide of sorts for you as you journey up the mountain or perhaps through the valley of this season in search of glory. I will provide you with stories and passages to study. I will ask you questions in a journaling style to give you freedom to reflect, explore, write lists or discover the way you feel led. The goal is not just to find specific answers but to dig into the scriptures and see where God leads you.

I will share with you a playlist of music and journal pages to record your own observed "glory moments." Together we will explore 8 sub-topics/themes, including creation, presence, worship, fame, suffering, community, justice and heaven to help us uncover the meaning of glory. Strap on your backpack. Fill up a water bottle. Grab your favorite pen, your Bible and perhaps a stash of good chocolate. It's time to begin chasing His glory.

As we move into this experience together, I'd like to challenge you to begin the first steps of this journey with prayer. The start of a hike or a run is often the hardest as we try to adjust to the terrain, use our muscles in a new way and steady our breathing. If prayer is not already a daily habit, set an alarm on your phone or a timer in your kitchen. Choose 5, 10, 30 minutes a day that will be your time to sit—not just to talk, but to listen to God. Got kids clamoring for your attention? Go take a walk. Hide in your closet or bathroom. Wondering how you'll carve out the time? Make your commute a sacred space for prayer. Lacking inspiration? Listen for the whisper. Tune your heart strings to the music He is playing just for you. Write down your thought-prayers.

Questions to reflect on:

1. What do you already know about glory? What images (secular or sacred) does this word stir up for you?

2. What do you want to invest in this experience?

3. What do you want to gain from this experience?

4. What is something broken in you where you long to see His glory?

Bonus Glory

This study is designed to be interactive on many levels. My hope and prayer is that you will be called to engage in God's Word in new ways through this study. I invite you to take the posture of an active learner. My challenge to you is to venture out beyond the well-worn, familiar path to explore new media and exercise some new spiritual muscles as you learn to become a Glory Chaser.

This workbook includes pages for "Glimpses of glory" you can record throughout the week as well as pages for "Notes" from the lecture or prayer requests if you are doing this with a friend or group of friends. I also encourage you to start a Facebook group or establish another way of connecting online throughout the week if you're doing this in community. This can be a place to post "bonus glory" links. These might be quotes, sermons, videos or additional songs that can offer further study and inspiration to chase God's glory in the day-to-day. My desire is to add layers to the study and allow all different types of learners a chance to engage further. This supplementary material is not a requirement to complete the study. Consider it a bonus!

I have created a playlist of worship music to accompany your study. Each song is connected to the overarching theme of glory and serves to help you delve deeper into the sub-themes of the study. At a basic level, you can listen to the music at your leisure. You might follow my "Glory Chasers" playlist on Spotify or download these songs on your iPhone, iPad, laptop or other device and listen to them throughout the specific week. You might choose to dig deeper by looking up the lyrics to each song and treat them as supplementary reading. Steeping yourself in the worship music could serve as an added dimension of exploration and study.

Notes

Glimpses of Glory

> **Bonus Glory:**
> "Glory is anything that is all God. It's God's goodness."
> —Beth Moore, *A Woman's Heart: God's Dwelling*

WEEK TWO
CREATION

I knew I only had a few minutes if I wanted to catch it. I started to jog faster. I climbed over rocks. I scrambled around strange bushes. My foot caught on something, and I stumbled. The darkness rushed in behind me, but I kept moving forward, sprinting now straight for that light. I finally made it to the top of the steep hill. Then I saw it—the view I had been anticipating all along. I sucked in a huge breath beholding that giant ball of orange-crimson-fiery sun floating over the expanse of ocean before me. So much bigger and more beautiful than I imagined. I tried to snap a few pictures, but they couldn't capture the depth and expanse of the landscape. They were but reflections of such a greater, fuller, more glorious beauty. The sun ball slipped ever-so-quickly into the coin slot of the horizon. My heart filled with a strange sadness to enjoy it for only seconds.

What came next was the real surprise. That's when I saw the real glory unfolding. The sky filled with ribbons of dancing color extending from that place where the sun had been. A deep merlot. A pumpkin orange and lemon yellow. A dusky lavender. I heard a symphony of ocean waves roaring below me. As the minutes ticked by, a heavy blanket of the purest, deepest indigo gently covered it all. A dot of moon hung in the distance. In that space, I could speak only one word: *glory*. It escaped like a whisper from my lips. This was His glory displayed just for me. I will always remember that moment. I was filled with this indescribable warmth, this gentle peace, this overwhelming sense that my Creator was there. After months of fighting back my worst fears and enduring such pain and sickness, death and grief, He was reaching out to me with the arms of a sunset and whispering, "I am here. I see you. I am unfolding something more glorious than you could ever imagine."

If we slow down our schedules, our bodies, our thoughts, our hearts, to take in the beauty of creation, we can't help but meet the one and only divine Creator. In Psalm 19:1, David writes, "The heavens declare the glory of God, and the sky proclaims the work of His hands." I suspect David had a sunset experience much like mine, by recognizing that creation is an arrow pointing us to God. Ann Voskamp explains it this way in her book, *One Thousand Gifts*: "Pantheism, seeing the natural world as divine, is a very different thing than seeing divine God present in all things. I know it here kneeling, the twilight so still: nature is not God but God is revealing the weight of Himself, all His glory through the looking glass of nature."[1]

There is far too much intricacy and detail and sheer beauty in the universe not to see Him there. I see His glory in the regal pine trees at Bass Lake pointing toward heaven. I see His glory in the breathtaking view of Half Dome in Yosemite National Park. I see His glory in the perfectly-formed lips of my newborn baby girl. I see His glory in the heavy fruit that springs from seemingly-dead grape vines—all in His time.

Recently I went to the Monterey Bay Aquarium with my daughters and some friends. I was captivated by the Jellies exhibit. These amazing marine animals are often called jellyfish, but they are not really fish. They have bodies that look like translucent umbrellas with decorative, curly tentacles that trail behind them like the train of a wedding dress. I could have spent hours just watching the jellies move. These creatures are more graceful than ballerinas. They sashay through the water by expanding and contracting their bell-shaped bodies to push water behind them. Scientists confirm that jellies are the most energy-efficient swimmers. Yet, they move in a slow-motion dance. They are not in a hurry.

My friend and I were talking about why God created jellies. In a practical sense, jellies are part of an elaborate ocean food chain. Bigger marine animals like tuna, sharks, swordfish and sea turtles eat jellies. They eat plants, fish eggs and larvae. Yet, I believe it is more than just a food chain thing. The grace and creativity of the jellies is about art. I can't help but think that an Artist-God created jellies to display His glory. In her book, *A Million Little Ways: Uncover the Art You Were Made to Live*, Emily P. Freeman writes, "In the beginning, God made art. His art marks the foundation of everything we know. The kind of art God makes is not an afterthought or a weekend hobby he does on the side. God's art is the starting point for the story of the world."[2] This quote reminds me of the intentionality of our Creator, the grand design of His Creation. He did not create things as purely functional. There is an element of art and appreciation to every piece of His Creation.

The Bible narrative commences in Genesis with the creation of the world. That's also where our glory story begins. This week we will look closely at the way our Creator created. I'm inviting you to chase His Glory with me through the lens of Creation. I challenge you to take time to study the scriptures, but also to observe His art. Even if you live in the city, I would guess there is some thing or some place you can find that displays His glory. Part of being a Glory Chaser is opening the eyes of our hearts in wonder to see something new, a greater story God is unfolding with details very personal to you. Press in. See what He reveals to you this week.

As I read and reread the account of Creation, which was written by Moses, I am most captivated by the way God created us. Lean into the text with me. "Then God said, 'Let Us make man in Our image, according to our likeness" (Genesis 1:26, HCSB). While all the rest of Creation was spoken into being, God gathered together in community (Father, Son, and Holy Spirit) to form us with his own hands from the earth. "Then the LORD God formed the man out of the dust from the ground and breathed the breath of life into his nostrils, and the man became a living being " (Genesis 2:7, HCSB). We might say God was the very first sculptor, using the dust-clay of the ground to form His masterpiece.

Part of the story is that God created us in His image to create. He created us as art to create art. I love the way Hank Fortener explains it in the sermon series, "The Artisan Soul." He says, "We are God's finest creation. He spends hundreds and thousands of years using art to create the conversation with humanity—using music to stop battles, using art to chase away evil spirits, using art to stop violence, and then you and I become the finest work of art… God says, 'You are my symphony.' You were prepared to be His workmanship."[3] This week I'm encouraging you to find your "artisan soul." Maybe you don't consider yourself an artist. Few of us do. We have lost our childlike wonder and freedom to create. We filter and edit ourselves. We spend too much time worrying about the art in the galleries and lining the bookstore shelves. We become paralyzed to live out what we were created to do.

What would change if making art was part of our job descriptions? How would we live differently if we believed God created us as artists to reflect His glory? What if we looked for ways He could help us make art out of our storied pasts, our gifts, our addictions, our daily conversations—all for His glory? Let's come back next week and unpack the answers to some of those questions.

Songs for worship & inspiration this week:

(See Spotify playlist "Glory Chasers")

"Show Me Your Glory" by Third Day
"Beautiful Things" by Gungor
"Glory in the Highest" by Chris Tomlin
"Rising Sun" by All Sons & Daughters
"Holy" by Matt Redman

Memory Verse:

The heavens declare the glory of God; the sky above proclaims his handiwork.
—Psalm 19:1 (ESV)

DAY ONE: GENESIS

We enter into the glory narrative in the book of Genesis. Pray for fresh eyes to read this story and see His glory in a new way. Read Genesis 1:1-2:25. While you're reading, circle key words and underline phrases that repeat in the rhythm of God's Creation. (Feel free to jot notes about your observations here.)

1. Make a quick reference chart of what God created on each day.

    DAY ONE

    _____

    DAY TWO

    _____

    DAY THREE

    _____

    DAY FOUR

    _____

    DAY FIVE

    _____

    DAY SIX

    _____

2. Note the specific and unique way God created humans. Who was involved in that creation process?

   _____

   _____

   _____

3. Reread Genesis 1:26-27. Look it up in at least 3 different versions of the Bible. If you've never done this before, you can use web sites like www.biblestudytools.com or www.blueletterbible.com, or the YouVersion Bible app to help you. What are some of the differences in language in the different versions you read?

   _____

   _____

   _____

4. God created men and women in his "image" or "likeness." This affirms that humans were created to represent or reflect God in a way unlike any other part of His creation. What does it mean to you that you are created in God's image?

   _____

   _____

   _____

DAY TWO: GOD AS ARTIST

Have you ever thought about God as an artist? Scanning the scriptures, we can see His work as a knitter, a dancer, a storyteller, a musician, a counselor, a street artist, a poet, a craftsman, a counselor. God created us in His image. He created us to create. We are artisans created in His image. I love the way Erwin McManus, author of *The Artisan Soul*, puts it: "The entire universe reflects God's essence. God creates out of who he is, and when we are aligned with him, everything we create brings him honor and glory."[4]

5. Explore some other stories that show God working as an artist. What kind of art does God use in these stories? How is this art used to bring God glory?

   *Joshua 6

   *1 Samuel 16:23

   *Nehemiah 3

   *Jeremiah 18

6. In Genesis 2:19-20, God gives Adam the creative work of naming all the living creatures. Think about your own name or the names of your children. What is significant about these names? How is naming something an act of creation?

_____

_____

_____

_____

DAY THREE: GOD'S CREATION

7. Take a 15-minute walk through the forest or run through the neighborhood or sit on your back porch. Take a drive up to the mountains or pause by the nearest lake or pond. Explore some of God's creation. Take note of the small details—the spine of a leaf, the trunk of a tree, your own fingerprint, the color palette of a sunset. Take some time to reflect what you see. Take a risk. Snap some photos. Write a poem. Paint a picture. Jot a list of all the examples of His Glory you see around you in nature. Challenge your artist self to create a reflection of God's Creation.

_____

_____

_____

_____

_____

Bonus Glory:

"Dusk and all the arching dome and the field and the great-bellied moon, it all heaves, heavy with the glory. I heave to breathe: The whole earth is full of His glory. Sky, land, and sea, heavy and saturated with God—why do I always forget?"

—Ann Voskamp,
One Thousand Gifts

DAY FOUR: PSALMS

8. Read Psalm 8. Circle the word "glory" as you read. Who is speaking?

   _____
   _____
   _____
   _____

9. Write about the way glory is used in this context. What are some synonyms you might use in place of the word glory in this Psalm?

   _____
   _____
   _____
   _____

10. How do you respond to what this Psalm is saying?

    _____
    _____
    _____
    _____
    _____

11. Read Psalm 29. Circle the word glory as you read. What is the tone of this Psalm? This Psalm talks a lot about how God has dominion over creation. Underline/jot down some example of these images.

_____

_____

_____

_____

_____

12. If we are created in God's image, what are the implications of this Psalm for us today?

_____

_____

_____

_____

_____

DAY FIVE: EPHESIANS

Emily P. Freeman writes in *A Million Little Ways*, "What if we decided to believe our purpose in this world really is to reflect the glory of God? Would we begin to see ourselves as wildly free, to approach the universe—the meal plan, the work project, the yard sale, our neighbor, the roof leak, the doctor appointment, the eternal destiny of our children—to approach it all with a wide-eyed wonder, with an edge-of-your-seat breath, with an expectation that any minute God will show himself in a way we have not yet seen? And he'll likely do it through us?"[5]

13. Read Ephesians 2:10. Write it out in your journal or in the space below.

14. How does this verse relate back to Freeman's point about our purpose?

15. How does this speak to where you are in your life today?

DAY SIX: JOURNAL & REFLECT

16. Reflect on your journey this week. Respond to one or all of these questions in the space below: What made the biggest impact on you? In what ways will you chase God's glory in Creation in the days to come? How can you discover His glory more regularly?

_____

_____

_____

_____

_____

_____

_____

_____

_____

_____

_____

CREATION

Glimpses of glory

Notes

WEEK THREE
PRESENCE

I was standing in the middle of the community garden with my daughter's second grade class when I received the phone call. My husband's voice on the other end was hushed, markedly different from his typically playful and loud coaching voice. Results of biopsy. Melanoma cancer. His diagnosis was a sucker punch to the gut. I stood there frozen somewhere between the rows of corn and kale, holding a diaper bag and several water bottles for the kids on the field trip. My healthy, athletic husband had cancer. At the prime-of-life-age of 40. I struggled to even breathe.

My mind swirled, but I was stress paralyzed. What should I do? Text our family? Call our life group? Cry? Sink into a heap in the dirt? Scream? Pray? Leave the kids and go to my man? Fear started to suffocate me. We had known for weeks that this strange bump had been growing on Ericlee's right hip. I witnessed his increasing discomfort in that area, but we believed what many had told us—it was a torn muscle. He had participated in several strenuous athletic events in the last year. A torn muscle made sense. I had never let my mind wander to the C-word.

When I walked with my daughter's class the few blocks back to the school, I tried to digest it all. My mind ping-ponged with questions: Was it treatable? Would it require surgery? Would Ericlee consider chemotherapy? Would our insurance cover this? Would I end up raising our three girls alone? Who would walk them down the aisle?

"Mom!" my eight-year-old's excited voice interrupted my thoughts. Hovering over a bush with the other kids huddled around her, she motioned me to join them. I entered the circle of kids full of wide-eyed wonder, and then I spotted it. A butterfly. With paper-thin wings of pale yellow outlined by inky black, it sat perfectly still on a leaf while the kids held their breath and took in all its glory.

Right there in downtown Fresno, with buses and cars careening past us, in the polluted air, with cracks in the sidewalk and trash in the streets, we had come face-to-face with God's glory. This was that perfectly-timed reminder that there is beauty when we press into the raw, the hard things, and the change. It seemed like such a small thing, but truly that moment was a big thing for me. Like that butterfly, I was about to endure a painful, yet beautiful metamorphosis. I felt God's Presence. I took a deep breath, and just for a few seconds, my questions calmed.

As I was driving home to be with my man after that field trip, the chorus of my new favorite song, "Oceans" by Hillsong United, started playing on the radio. I whispered the words, "Spirit, lead me where my Trust is without borders. Let me walk upon the waters wherever you would call me."[6] During one of the scariest moments of my life, I found myself singing. The presence of my Savior washed over me.

That difficult first night was filled with tears, prayers with our family, and wondering aloud where God was taking us. After all, we ran a busy nonprofit that ministered to people in Haiti. I directed a jewelry project with goods made by Haitian women. My husband and I already purchased our tickets to take four teams to Haiti that next month. We had three young daughters and lots of dreams for them and our future together. We didn't have time for cancer. The next morning I penned this raw prayer-poem to my Father:

Dear Lord,
Last night I did not believe.
I walked out toward the water and dove
right into
the crashing waves.
Waves of fear
Waves of regret
Waves of selfishness
Waves of betrayal
Waves of mistrust
Waves of abandonment
Waves of sorrow
All I could see were waves.
Barely breathing,
they smacked me one after the other and
I couldn't see you.
My eyes were stinging
and blurry with salt water.
Spirit, lead me out on the waters,
stepping above these waves.
Help me with my Unbelief, Lord.
Help me to look above those waves
and steady my eyes
on you.
Help me to tune my heart to yours.
It's so hard to see
to hear
to feel you now
when people ask questions, when we
all face these decisions, when I have to say no to all the
good things you have called me to.
My heart just trembles with all these questions. Teach me to trust.
Help me to praise you even in this storm.
You're enough for me.
Amen

> **Memory Verse**
>
> *Then Moses said, "Now show me your glory."*
> —Exodus 33:18 (NIV)

Looking back, I know it was an honest and bold prayer. I felt like David crying out to God in the Psalms. Just a month earlier I had been studying Psalm 139. David's words rang out: "I can never escape from your Spirit! I can never get away from your Presence! If I go up to heaven, you are there; if I go down to the grave, you are there. If I ride the wings of the morning, if I dwell by the farthest oceans, even there your hand will guide me, and your strength will support me" (v. 7-10). David recognizes God's "omnipresence," that God was and is everywhere. He could not escape God's Presence even if he wanted to, and he certainly did not. I found great comfort in knowing God was with me, ever-present.

I steeped myself in the words of that "Oceans" song over the next several months as we stepped out on the waters facing all the unknowns—as we visited doctors for treatment options, as we canceled our summer trip to Haiti, as we prayed and cried out to God for healing, as the cancer spread throughout Ericlee's lymph nodes and to his lungs, as I eventually had to make the hard phone call to hospice. There were many days I felt surrounded by darkness but His Presence proved that ever-present glimmer of light and hope. His glory abounded in the deepest waters.

The word "glory" comes from the Latin word "gloria," meaning fame, renown, honor, divine quality, unspoken manifestation of God, splendor, majesty, brightness.[7] In the King James Version, the word "glory" is mentioned 538 times. Glory has several meanings, but it is often used in reference to God's Presence and a brilliance or light. This week we will be exploring the unique ways different men and women of the Bible experienced God's Presence. Let's first dive into the book of Exodus and take a front row seat to the dramatic story of Moses as he encounters God's Presence in very visible and tangible ways. Exodus 29:43 says this: "I will meet the people of Israel there, in the place made holy by my glorious presence." (NLT) He meets us where we are with His glory. He makes even the darkest places light and holy.

Then we will discover with Elijah how God speaks through a whisper and reminds us of His Presence in unexpected ways. I urge you to journey with Mary, the mother of God, who also experiences His Presence in a unique way. We will close the week by pondering how God sent us his Son as a physical presence and later the Holy Spirit as a spiritual presence to point us toward His glory. I have come to understand His Presence as the greatest gift.

Songs for worship & inspiration this week:

(See Spotify playlist "Glory Chasers")

"Oceans (Where Feet May Fail)" by Hillsong United
"Show Me Your Glory" by Jesus Culture
"Mother of God" by The Brilliance
"God With Us" by All Sons & Daughters
"Light of the World" by Lauren Daigle
"Holy Spirit" by Francesca Battistelli

> **Bonus Glory:**
> *"The Holy Spirit desires that our self be completely submerged—not merely ankle-deep, knee-deep, waist-deep, but self-deep. He wants us hidden and bathed under this life-giving stream. Let loose the lines holding you to the shore and sail into the deep. And never forget, the Man who does the measuring is with us today."*
> —J. Gresham Machen, *Streams in the Desert*

DAY ONE: MOSES

For today, we are going to camp in the book of Exodus. Start by reading Exodus 14. You might also consider listening to this chapter through the YouVersion Bible app. This section tells about how the Israelites crossed the Red Sea." Put on your "glory lens" and see what you discover.

17. What do you learn about God's glory and Presence in this chapter?

   _____

   _____

   _____

18. Take special note of the relationship between Moses and God. How do the people react to Moses and God. Did they trust and feel God's Presence themselves?

   _____

   _____

   _____

19. One of the primary ways God's glory or presence is with Moses and the people throughout the book of Exodus is through a cloud. Read the following passages and jot down a few phrases or sentences describing how you envision that cloud experience in light of what is written.

Exodus 19:9

_____

Exodus 20:21-22

_____

Exodus 24:15-18

_____

Exodus 40:34-38

_____

20. In Exodus 33:22-23 it says, "As my glorious presence passes by, I will hide you in the crevice of the rock and cover you with my hand until I have passed by. Then I will remove my hand and let you see me from behind. But my face will not be seen." Can you think of a way you have personally experienced God's presence covering you or seeing it from behind?

_____

_____

_____

_____

_____

DAY TWO: ELIJAH

The prophet Elijah experienced God's Presence in powerful, yet unexpected ways. Read 1 Kings 17:8-24.

21. How did God provide for Elijah through the widow at Zarephath?

22. How did Elijah experience God's Presence there?

23. Elijah enters into a showdown on the top of Mount Carmel to show God's glory to King Ahab, Queen Jezebel and the people. Elijah calls on God to go up against the prophets of Baal. This required great courage. How does God's Presence appear in 1 Kings 18:17-46?

24. After Elijah experienced such a dramatic display of God's glory at the top of Mount Carmel, he still experiences fear and doubt. How does God reveal himself very personally to Elijah in 1 Kings 19:1-15?

_____

_____

_____

_____

_____

25. Have you ever had this kind of unexpected encounter with God?

_____

_____

_____

_____

_____

DAY THREE: MARY

Christmas is the time we celebrate the coming of Emmanuel. Even the very name "Emmanuel" means "God with us." God sent his son as a physical Presence to be with His people on earth. Mary, the mother of Jesus, is the first to enter into God's Presence as she births God's Son. Choose a translation of the Bible you don't normally read and reread Luke 2:1-20.

26. Take some time to write about how you imagine Mary's experience. What emotions do you think Mary felt as she went through this process?

27. How does she enter into His Presence?

DAY FOUR: JESUS

28. Jesus was sent to earth as a physical expression of God's Presence. God "glorified" His Son. He named Him "Emmanuel," meaning "God with us." Read the following verses and draw some connections for yourself about God's Presence as manifested through His Son:

Hebrews 1:1-3

_____

_____

Matthew 28:20

_____

_____

John 1:14

_____

_____

John 17:5

_____

_____

29. Write a prayer asking Emmanuel to be with you in your present circumstances?

DAY FIVE: HOLY SPIRIT

After Jesus ascended, God sent the Holy Spirit as a teacher, counselor, advocate, comforter, inspiration and intercessor to dwell within us. Read John 14:16-26.

30. How does this passage describe the Holy Spirit?

31. What has shaped your ideas or experiences with the Holy Spirit in your life?

32. Spend some time writing about how the Holy Spirit has been present with you. List a few specific examples of how you felt the Holy Spirit working this week.

DAY SIX: JOURNAL & REFLECT

33. Take some time to reflect on your journey this week. Respond to one or more of the following questions: What made the biggest impact on you? In what ways will you intentionally enter into His presence this week? How will you chase God's glory in your everyday rhythms?

Notes

Glimpses of Glory

WEEK FOUR
WORSHIP

When I was in college, I sang in two choirs. The first was a women's choir made up of mostly freshmen and sophomores. Our director, Merle, was as dramatic and unique as his name might suggest. He was precise in his direction and a lover of classical music. We spent hours reading sheet music, practicing each part, and listening to the enunciation of each word in romantic languages. We practiced opening our mouths wider for fuller sound and standing perfectly poised for concerts.

Merle was no-nonsense. Since we were all coming from varying degrees of vocal training, his goal was to reign us in. He cared deeply about the presentation. I loved being a part of this choir because I got to participate in something so much bigger than myself. I was a second soprano and my part was only as important as I was willing to blend my voice with the other dozens of women who showed up for rehearsals. When we were on stage together donning our formal attire, I remember feeling like I was part of an angel choir. I had the privilege of standing down in front because I am short. This meant I was surrounded by the myriad voices mixing and sailing out to the auditorium. This was a pure worship, so different from what I knew in church.

The second choir I joined was the Gospel Choir. We met on Sunday afternoons and there I experienced something entirely different and new. Our director was curly-haired and full of passion. She swung the doors wide

> **Memory Verse:**
>
> *Sing to the LORD, bless his name; tell of his salvation from day to day. Declare his glory among the nations, his marvelous works among all the peoples!*
>
> —Psalm 96:2-3 (ESV)

open to anyone who wanted to be a part of the choir. She expected excellence from all of us. Gospel Choir required an entirely different skill set. There was no sheet music. Our director and leaders modeled the notes and melodies for us. In traditional call and response gospel style, they would sing a run and we would repeat it. The repertoire consisted of a diversity of music—everything from anthems, to jazz, to spirituals, to contemporary gospel music.

I found myself timid in this choir at first. Our director wanted us to sing loud and with feeling. My classically-trained voice struggled to free itself, to take flight. As the weeks flew by, I learned to love Gospel Choir. I loved the energy, the mix of music and new friends from all different backgrounds and creeds. I was never the star chosen for solos or singled out to lead a section, but I gained so much from diving into that experience as a participant. I loved to listen to my talented friends hover and dance over the notes. I loved to close my eyes and get lost in the music. I learned to worship in a new way.

I share these two choir experiences because they taught me something so elemental about worship. It's a lesson I learned over and over again as I have traveled to countries like Costa Rica, Guatemala, Nicaragua, Spain, and Haiti and experienced so many different cultures and styles of worship. It's a lesson emphasized to me as I have visited churches across the United States with all kinds of different values about music. I have learned that Worship can and should be experienced in many ways. In fact, the diversity of ways God's people sing and play music is pleasing to Him.

Music has the power to soothe and calm hearts. Music has the power to speak peace and comfort and truth. Music has the power to cross cultural lines. Music is one avenue to worship, bringing Glory to God. I often think about what it will be like to be in heaven one day with all the diversity of worship styles colliding and blending into one great choir or orchestra of sound.

David was called a man after God's heart. He was the author and composer of many of the Psalms, which were designed primarily for the people of God to worship together. Many of these psalms were used in the temple for worship. The book of Psalms is a love story, a collection of songs, a testament to God's Presence with His people. The Psalms are evidence that His Word is a fountain of worship. Psalm 115 reminds us that our life goal should be to give God glory. It's so easy for glory to get twisted and point back to ourselves. Psalm 115: 1 says, "Not to us, O LORD, but to you goes all the glory for your unfailing love and faithfulness" (New Living Translation). When we worship God, we bring him our confessions, our prayers, our thanks, our hopes, our dreams, our acts of service and we return them to Him.

Although music is one amazing way we can enter into a place of worship with our hearts, I believe worship is much bigger than music. The English word "worship" means "to ascribe worth to something." Worship is an invitation to commune with our Creator. Worship is a way we can individually and collectively ascribe worth to God or bring God glory. It is an active prayer to Him, an expression of our praise and adoration when we have experienced His Presence. Worship is an act of thanksgiving, an expression of our gratefulness for His grace and all the gifts he gives us.

I love to cook. I like to joke that cooking is my therapy. There is something about the act of chopping onions finely or mixing up a béchamel or the aromatic wonder of adding spices to the pot that centers me. Cooking affords me a space for being both quiet and creative. My kids might be screaming in the background, laundry might be taking over my couch, the pile of papers to grade might be growing , but when I get in the kitchen to cook dinner I get lost. In a good way. In that place, I can ponder all these things God is doing in my heart like Mary did. I can talk with Him. I can question.

The goal this week is to expand our definition and understanding of worship. Get ready for a wild and wonder-filled treasure hunt. In our first week, we contemplated the meaning of glory. I challenged you to delve into His creation, looking for Him all around us. Together we gained an understanding of ourselves as image bearers of God created for the purpose of reflecting His Glory. Last week, I invited you to enter into His Presence, to trace ways He has proved Emmanuel (God With Us) in the everyday. This week I urge you to press in to respond to His creation and presence through worship. As you do dishes, head out on your morning commute, listen to music, care for your family, or even exercise, I urge you to think about how all these things might be transformed into an act of worship for His glory.

Songs for worship & inspiration this week:

(See Spotify playlist "Glory Chasers")

"One Desire" by Kari Jobe
"Just Want to Praise You" by Maurette Clark Brown
"Your Glory/Nothing But the Blood" by All Sons & Daughters
"Calling on Fire" by Bellarive
"Glorious" (featuring Katie Torwalt) by Jesus Culture
"Be Thou My Vision" by Ascend the Hill

DAY ONE: MUSIC AS WORSHIP

34. Take some time today to think about the word "worship." What does it mean to you? What are some experiences you have had in your life that have been powerful times of worship? This week I invite you to carve out some concentrated time to listen to our "Glory Chasers" playlist. Choose one of the songs mentioned on this week's list of songs or another one that has really spoken to your heart. Print out the lyrics. Tape them to your mirror or keep a copy in your car. Steep yourself in this song. Use it as an avenue to enter into worship this week. Bring a copy of this song to share with our group or write the words of the chorus below.

DAY TWO: WHEN ANGELS SING

35. Last week I had you revisit the Christmas story, reading Luke 2:1-20. I want you to return to that story again but specifically keying into Luke 2:13-20. What did the angels do? What did they say?

36. How did they set the tone for worship of the newborn king?

37. How did the shepherds react?

38. Can you think of other examples in the Bible when people or angels reacted to an event with worship?

_____

_____

_____

DAY THREE: PSALM 96

Keep in mind that most of the Psalms were song lyrics—in many cases prayers set to music. Read Psalm 96.

39. What is the overall message of the lyrics of this song?

_____

_____

_____

40. What are some of the words or themes that emerge from this Psalm?

_____

_____

_____

41. What does this Psalm say to you about worship?

42. Contemplate these personal questions: How can I worship God daily with my thought life and even in the mundane tasks?

43. How can I make worship my immediate response when life's surprises and challenges come my way?

DAY FOUR: SAMARITAN WOMAN

Read the story of the Samaritan Woman at the Well in John 4:1-26. Take special note of Jesus' words to her in verses 21-24 that talk about worship.

44. Write out John 4:22-23 in the space below.

45. Circle the two words Jesus uses to express what worship should look like.

46. What do you think it means to worship in "spirit and truth"?

47. Why were these words Jesus spoke to the woman so important?

DAY FIVE: UNEXPECTED WORSHIP

48. Write out 1 Corinthians 10:31 in the space below. How is the word "glory" used in this scripture?

_____
_____
_____
_____

49. How is it part of our mandate as Christians to give God glory through worship?

_____
_____
_____
_____

50. List some examples of how you might worship in unexpected ways, places, or circumstances.

_____
_____
_____
_____

DAY SIX: JOURNAL & REFLECT

51. Reflect on your journey this week. Answer one ore more of the following questions: What made the biggest impact on you? In what ways will you discover His glory through different styles of worship? How will you make worship a lifestyle?

Bonus Glory:

"Worship is supernatural whenever people come hungry to respond, react, and receive from God for who He is and what He has done. A church worshipping as a Creature of the Word doesn't show up to perform or be entertained; she comes desperate and needy, thirsty for grace, receiving from the Lord and the body of Christ, and then gratefully receiving what she needs as she offers her praise-the only proper response to the God who saves us."

—Matt Chandler, *Creature of the Word: The Jesus-Centered Church*

Notes

Glimpses of glory

WEEK FIVE
FAME

We have an obsession in our culture with fame. Just say names like Oprah, Madonna, Bono, LeBron and immediately we conjure up certain images. If someone has a trace of talent or charisma, we transform them into a celebrity. Fame has become synonymous with glamour, glitz, riches, success and power. We elevate the lives of politicians, artists, rock stars, the rich and the famous. In recent years, we have brought the term "rock star" into our everyday lingo. Girls wear sparkly shirts that have the words "rock star" stamped across the front of them. Nail salons boast giving "rock star" pedicures. The fashion, cars and even the personal lives of celebrities have moved front and center in our culture. Through advertising and media, we are taught to emulate them.

The word "glory" in the Bible also points to this notion of fame. As mentioned before in the previous chapter, the Latin, "gloria" is used as a synonym for words, such as: fame, renown, praise, honor, and ambition. Our modern-day vernacular includes words and phrases like "glory days" to refer to the best years, the season full of success or the height of a person's career. We say things like: "He was in his glory when he made the winning shot of the game." In short, he felt great contentment, pride or happiness at that moment. These words and phrases help point to our notions of fame as part of the theme of glory.

> **Memory Verse:**
> "*I have appointed you for the very purpose of displaying my power in you, and to spread my fame throughout the whole earth.*"
> —Romans 9:17 (NLT)

One key element to a person's fame is their following. If a person gains a large following of people, they become famous. This is not necessarily a negative thing, unless, of course, that fame leads down a path of personal glorification. All too often humans have gained glory and it goes awry. Preacher and author John Piper explains, "Man was made to rely on God and give him glory. Instead man chose to rely on himself and seek his own glory—to make a name for himself."[8] This is the tension we must always fight—giving glory to ourselves or giving glory to God.

What would happen if the narrative was different? What would happen if we decided to tell a different story with our lives? When my husband and I first started dating, there was a worship song that became popular called "Famous One." We used to turn up that song loud, roll down the windows and sing it at the top of our lungs in the car together. It was different and catchy. One day a friend said, "Why do you like that song so much? I don't even get it." That's when I really started thinking about why Jesus was the "famous One."

I can hear Chris Tomlin singing these words in that song: "You are the one, the famous One, the famous One/ The heavens declare you're glorious, you're glorious/ Great is your fame beyond the earth."[9] This song is an anthem, a declaration, a love song to God naming Him as the famous One. He is above all of history's kings and all our present-day celebrities. All Creation and all of Heaven points to His glory and fame.

Several years after this song came out, Ericlee and I had the chance to take a class together called "Perspectives on the World Christian Movement." This course opened my eyes to the idea that we are all called to join God on a greater mission. One of my favorite guest speakers in that class was a petite woman with gleaming, dark eyes who delivered a powerful lesson on how God chose each one of us to be a part of "The Story of His Glory." She took us on a journey from Genesis to Revelation, showing how God's purpose is to overcome evil by redeeming people. His plan is to reveal Himself and establish His name among each and every one of the people groups scattered across the earth that they might worship and obey Him.

We have the exciting opportunity to be a part of that story. As we explored in Week One, God created us to be image bearers to reflect His Glory. We have an inherent glory in us because we are made in His image. This means we may taste His glory in a myriad of ways here on earth, but we must also be careful to take these things and use them as arrows pointing back to Him. In other words, we were created to make Him famous.

Part of the way we tell the Glory Story is by using our creativity to write, paint, craft conversations, do our jobs with excellence and even raise children in such a way that bears witness to the Glory Story. We have the opportunity to continue the glory narrative in the circles and spaces God has put us in.

In her book, *Known and Loved*, Caryn Rivadeneira writes, "We can see God in our stories. Which is why we're called to be storytellers. To tell others the stories of our lives—about the things we have endured and survived, the areas where we've failed and succeeded, and the times we've questioned and doubted. Because in all of these stories, others can see what God has done for us. And we can see it too."[10] Rivadeneira reminds us that each one of us is called to be a storyteller. This week I want you to think about creative ways you can share your story of His glory.

Ever since I was a little girl, I have wanted to be a writer. My first grade teacher, Mrs. Kosinski, is the first person who spoke words of encouragement to me about writing. I remember I wrote a story about two unicorns who fell in love and lived happily ever after. I added lots of description and illustrations to my story. I bravely named the boy unicorn after the boy in first grade whom I had a crush on. Mrs. Kosinski wrote "How romantic!" in the margin in red pen. She proceeded to put my story on the bulletin board in the hallway so everyone in the entire school could read my poorly-disguised story about my first-grade-crush. Perhaps the most important part of that memory is that Mrs. Kosinski planted a seed in me all those years ago. She made me believe I was created to be a storyteller.

You might not consider yourself a writer but you, too, were designed to tell God's Glory Story. Last week I challenged you to expand your definition of worship. This week let's contemplate the idea that we are designed to share our stories as an act of worship to bring God fame and glory. At the heart of every good story is a character who wants something and overcomes conflict to get it. Through the stories of Joseph, Esther, Isaiah, David and Paul, press in to see what you can learn about how fame is important to our study of glory.

Songs for worship & inspiration this week:

(See Spotify playlist "Glory Chasers")

"The Reason I Sing" by Jimmy Needham
"Famous One" by Chris Tomlin
"King of Glory" by Third Day
"Glory" by Hillsong Worship
"King of Glory" by Chris Tomlin

DAY ONE: JOSEPH

One of my favorite stories in the Bible is the story of Joseph. It's full of interesting characters, drama, deceit, famine and forgiveness. God designs Joseph's life story according to His plan to spread His glory among all the nations. He is with Joseph through character-building trials and then grants Joseph favor and fame in a unique way. Read Genesis 41:25-57.

52. How does God use Joseph to bless the surrounding countries and to introduce Himself as the "God of Joseph"?

53. What were Joseph's privileges, skills or spiritual gifts? How did these help him become famous?

54. How did Joseph use his skills and privileges to help Pharoah? His family? Others?

DAY TWO: ESTHER

Esther was perhaps the most unlikely candidate to be in a place of royalty and fame. She was an orphan. She was a woman. She was a Jew. Yet, God brings her into a royal position for "such a time as this" to save her people. If you have never read the story before, I encourage you to spend some time in this book today. Start by reading Esther 1:1-18.

55. Briefly describe in the space below how Esther rises to a royal position and the fame Esther experiences because of her new position.

56. Read Esther 6, and then describe the fame and glory Haman is fighting for in this chapter. In other words, what kind of fame is he after?

57. Have you ever felt like you needed to fight to get credit for something you did? What was that like?

58. Has God ever given you favor in an unexpected way that presented an avenue to bring Him glory?

_____

_____

_____

_____

_____

DAY THREE: THE GLORY STORY

59. The Bible includes a greater mandate for God's people to share the Glory Story with the nations. This brings us beyond the inward-focus of personal fame and opens our eyes to a greater purpose on earth. Isaiah 60 celebrates the glorious reversal of darkness. This section is often subtitled, "The Glory of Zion." In the lines of this prophecy, there is a global view—a vision for all nations experiencing His glory. Read Isaiah 60:1-22 below and circle all the times the word "glory" is used. Underline all the uses of the word "nations."

1 Arise, shine, for your light has come, and the glory of the LORD rises upon you.

2 See, darkness covers the earth and thick darkness is over the peoples, but the LORD rises upon you and his glory appears over you.

3 Nations will come to your light, and kings to the brightness of your dawn.

4 *"Lift up your eyes and look about you: All assemble and come to you; your sons come from afar, and your daughters are carried on the hip.*

5 *Then you will look and be radiant, your heart will throb and swell with joy; the wealth on the seas will be brought to you, to you the riches of the nations will come.*

6 *Herds of camels will cover your land, young camels of Midian and Ephah. And all from Sheba will come, bearing gold and incense and proclaiming the praise of the LORD.*

7 *All Kedar's flocks will be gathered to you, the rams of Nebaioth will serve you; they will be accepted as offerings on my altar, and I will adorn my glorious temple.*

8 *"Who are these that fly along like clouds, like doves to their nests?*

9 *Surely the islands look to me; in the lead are the ships of Tarshish, bringing your children from afar, with their silver and gold, to the honor of the LORD your God, the Holy One of Israel, for he has endowed you with splendor.*

10 *"Foreigners will rebuild your walls, and their kings will serve you. Though in anger I struck you, in favor I will show you compassion.*

11 *Your gates will always stand open, they will never be shut, day or night, so that people may bring you the wealth of the nations— their kings led in triumphal procession.*

12 *For the nation or kingdom that will not serve you will perish; it will be utterly ruined.*

13 "The glory of Lebanon will come to you, the juniper, the fir and the cypress together, to adorn my sanctuary; and I will glorify the place for my feet.

14 The children of your oppressors will come bowing before you; all who despise you will bow down at your feet and will call you the City of the LORD, Zion of the Holy One of Israel.

15 "Although you have been forsaken and hated, with no one traveling through, I will make you the everlasting pride and the joy of all generations.

16 You will drink the milk of nations and be nursed at royal breasts. Then you will know that I, the LORD, am your Savior, your Redeemer, the Mighty One of Jacob.

17 Instead of bronze I will bring you gold, and silver in place of iron. Instead of wood I will bring you bronze, and iron in place of stones. I will make peace your governor and well-being your ruler.

18 No longer will violence be heard in your land, nor ruin or destruction within your borders, but you will call your walls Salvation and your gates Praise.

19 The sun will no more be your light by day, nor will the brightness of the moon shine on you, for the LORD will be your everlasting light, and your God will be your glory.

20 Your sun will never set again, and your moon will wane no more; the LORD will be your everlasting light, and your days of sorrow will end.

21 Then all your people will be righteous and they will possess the land forever. They are the shoot I have planted, the work of my hands, for the display of my splendor.

22 The least of you will become a thousand, the smallest a mighty nation. I am the LORD; in its time I will do this swiftly. (NIV)

60. What do you think is the message in Isaiah 60 about glory and the nations?

_____
_____
_____
_____
_____
_____
_____
_____

> **Bonus Glory:**
> "Do you want to impact other people's lives? Do you want your life to be changed? Or do you just want to make a name for yourself? Is this about God's glory, or is it about self-promotion?... These questions matter because we'll soon learn —one way or another—that there's a cost to discipleship."
> —Eugene Cho, *Overrated*

DAY FOUR: HIS GLORY OR MINE?

61. My husband had a stack of 3x5 notecards that he kept in his top left desk drawer. These notecards were full of hand-scrawled, inspiring quotes he had jotted down in different seasons of his life. This one caught my attention: Does my life cause people to praise God or me? Take some time to reflect on this in light of our conversation about fame and glory. How does this question challenge you and inspire you where you are sitting right now?

DAY FIVE: PAUL

Paul caught the vision for spreading the Glory Story to the nations. In his many travels, Paul was called to the ancient city of Athens, which was settled before 3000 B.C. and named for Athena, the goddess of wisdom. Athens was regarded in Paul's day as the intellectual capital of the world and known for its art, literature and philosophy. Paul addresses the people in the middle of the Areopagus (also known as Mars Hill, the oldest and most famous court in Athens).

62. Read Acts 17:24-31. Keep in mind this audience had no concept of God or the Old Testament. How would you describe the opening to Paul's address?

___

63. How does Paul appeal to his audience or speak directly to them in these verses?

___

64. How does Paul use this opportunity to share the glory story?

65. Do you have any personal examples of times where you were called to share the gospel in a totally different culture or for a different audience?

DAY SIX: JOURNAL & REFLECT

66. Journal and reflect on your journey this week. Answer one or more of the following questions: What made the biggest impact on you? In what ways do you see yourself participating in His Glory Story? How will you work to make God famous in your family, community, circle of influence?

_____

_____

_____

_____

_____

_____

_____

_____

_____

_____

_____

_____

Notes

Glimpses of glory

WEEK SIX
SUFFERING

I pulled out the left desk drawer in search of the calculator. This desk was his desk. Medium- brown oak, sturdy, timeless. We hauled this desk from the old house to storage at a friend's house, then out of storage, and then into our current rental home. Three guys muscled that thing through the yard and in through the back door. This desk is now my work space although you might not be able tell. Several months after my beloved graduated into Glory, the drawers are still stuffed with his things—a letter opener, spiral notebooks, a mini screwdriver, an international calling card, phone numbers jotted on pieces of paper, his wallet, old checkbook registers, a Ziploc bag full of change.

I opened the drawer and there on the top was a stack of 3-by-5 cards neatly clipped together. These words in his familiar scrawl jumped off the card straight into my heart:

Seldom will there be a more opportune time to share about God than when you are suffering and glorifying Him through it.

He had underlined the words "suffering" and "glorifying Him." I fingered the stack of notecards, noticing the yellowed edges. The date in the corner was March 1, 1996, but I knew in my heart it was no accident that I was pulling the card out of the drawer for the first time on September 27, 2014 —exactly 18 days after his death. It was like a postcard from heaven. In

> **Memory Verse:**
>
> *Dear Friends, do not be surprised at the fiery ordeal that has come on you to test you, as though something strange were happening to you. But rejoice inasmuch as you participate in the sufferings of Christ, so that you may be overjoyed when his glory is revealed.*
>
> —1 Peter 4:12-13 (NIV)

the midst of my deep grief and suffering, Ericlee was reminding me that I had a platform, an opportunity to share our story and bring God glory. It still gives me goose bumps to think about the way he continues to coach me from heaven.

I do not want to write a chapter on suffering. I don't. Just typing the word makes me shudder in my spirit. I'd much rather write about chocolate or dreams or hope or something more festive. Yet deep in my soul I know that a study about glory would never be complete if I did not brave the topic that has taught me the most profound lessons. Charles Spurgeon wrote, "Those who dive in the sea of affliction bring up rare pearls."[12] This past year has been a season for diving into suffering, but coming up with many surprising glimpses of His glory.

I have seen and experienced a fair amount of death and suffering in my life. When I was in fourth grade I lost my beloved Grandpa John, who died of a massive heart attack. This was my first dance with death. My memories are vivid from that time. I remember the hotel we stayed in near the funeral home. I remember the smell of the Bob Evans restaurant where we ate most of our meals because no one had the energy to cook. I remember my grandma wailing and clinging to the casket—this the second husband she would bury.

I remember the heavy weight on my own young heart to lose my grandpa—my hero, mentor and friend. This was my sweet Grandpa, who used to hold me on his knee and pinch my cheeks and call me a "hard head" in Italian. As a young person, I had to dive into the idea of death and losing someone very close to me. A few years later, my favorite cousin, Raymond, was killed in a tragic car accident. His life was also ripped away suddenly, but because he was so young and seemed to have his whole life ahead of him his death seemed more of a shock. As a seventh grader, I began to cry out to God. I began to question in my grief. What was the purpose? Why would God allow such tragedy? Why do we have to endure suffering?

Throughout my life, I have witnessed suffering in many forms. I have walked through the largest garbage dump in Central America and watched Guatemalan children digging through the scraps for their morning meal. I have looked long into the eyes of a young Haitian boy dying of tuberculosis. I experienced a physical assault in college that resulted in years of mental suffering as I battled fear and anxiety. I have walked with friends and family facing infertility, abuse, divorce, death of children, rape, chronic pain and mental illness. God has given me a heart of mercy so when I hear about reports of racial riots in Ferguson or young girls lured into sex-trafficking in Nepal, I am deeply affected. The pain is mine; the suffering feels real.

The Hebrew word for glory is "kâbôd," meaning "someone or something that is heavy in weight, wealth, abundance, importance or respect." This definition reminds me that glory is not just about creation, presence, worship and fame. The concept of glory also possesses a kind of weightiness, a heaviness. There is a deep sense of responsibility in glory. There is also a sense of sacrifice, a leaning toward loss, and a message of redemption. This is where suffering moves to center stage in our life drama. Suffering becomes a hallway leading us to glory and into Glory on the other side. Without suffering, we cannot experience the "beauty from ashes" narrative God is writing. Without suffering, we cannot understand the sacrifice of our Savior on the cross. Without suffering, we may never have an opportunity to enter into the dark places and journey with others who need community.

When my beloved was diagnosed with stage four melanoma cancer, I began to understand the deepest weight of suffering. The ache felt heavier than any suffering I had tasted or witnessed before. I remember that Saturday after the doctor called, my parents offered to take our kids and we drove to a local park. Ericlee and I spread a blanket out on the rough grass and laid down under a tree. We looked up at the branches and beyond to the heavens. I trembled and clung to him. We cried. We tried to digest what this could mean. The C-word felt so big and overwhelming and ominous. Stage four felt like a certain stamp of death.

We pressed repeat on a song by the band Shane & Shane called "Though You Slay Me," featuring an excerpt from John Piper. The chorus of the song includes words straight from the book of Job, "Though you slay me, yet I will praise you. Though you take from me, I will bless your name. Though you ruin me, still I will worship—sing a song to the one who's all I need..." We struggled through those words but we sang them with cracking voices together under the arms of that great tree. I had no concept of the physical suffering that was to come for my beloved, but I heard the words of the song and Piper's preaching. I began to believe that whatever suffering we were to endure was an opportunity to point others to God. Ericlee talked to me about the faith of his heroes Abraham, Moses and Noah—how they had to step out into the unknown trusting God for the unthinkable, the impossible. We had to believe as Piper preached that every tear would be worth it all, every millisecond of pain in the path of obedience was purposeful and producing an eternal glory.[13]

Everything about the cancer journey felt like a surprise. Yet I have been reminded time and again that none of it was a surprise to my God. When it comes down to it, none of it should have been a real surprise to me either. The Bible is full of stories and warnings about trials and suffering. 1 Peter 4:12-13 says, "Dear friends, do not be surprised at the fiery ordeal that has come on you to test you, as though something strange were happening to you. But rejoice inasmuch as you participate in the suffering of Christ, so that you may be overjoyed when His glory is revealed." I do not find one single promise in the Bible that says we will be exempt from suffering. Believe me, I've looked. Instead I find verse after verse that urges us to expect suffering, to embrace suffering, to count it a privilege that we get to enter into partnership with Jesus Christ. Suffering is a part of the plan of redemption.

In his book, Feed My Sheep, John Piper writes, "The suffering of sickness and the suffering of persecution have this in common: they are both intended by Satan for the destruction of our faith, and governed by God for the purifying of our faith... Christ sovereignly accomplishes His loving, purifying purpose, by overruling Satan's destructive attempts. Satan is always aiming to destroy our faith; but Christ magnifies His power in weakness."[14] At every junction of our journey, we must make a choice. We can continue down a road of despair where Satan would like to lead me or we can pray for God's power to be made real through our weaknesses. We can pray for opportunities to reflect His glory even in the gravest of circumstances.

Is it any coincidence the word "passion" originates in the Latin word "passionem," which means "to suffer"?[15] If I am passionate about my faith, I must step forward with a willingness to suffer. It's counter-intuitive, but it's the crux of our faith. Through suffering, we experience the sacrifice of Christ and gain His attributes with no greater opportunity to bring Him glory. Even Jesus longed for a different path, a different way to achieve glory for all of us. The words of his prayer to the Father echo throughout eternity: "Father, if you are willing, please take this cup of suffering away from me. Yet I want your will to be done, not mine" (Luke 22:42, NLT).

The good news is: suffering is not the end of the story. Jesus died, but then three days later he rose from the dead. No sin has the power to separate us anymore. He was the Redeemer—the one who through death brought new value to my life and yours. He threw open the doors of eternity for us all.

As you step into this week studying glory and suffering, I beg you not to shy away. I urge you to press in to hear what God has for you. What I have personally experienced in the space of deep suffering and loss is the most precious, the most powerful evidence of God and His glory. Like Hagar, Job and Paul, I long for you to taste it too, my friends. I return to the 3-by-5 card I found in the desk drawer. Through that little card, Ericlee spoke courage, grace, and life over me, reminding me of my purpose.

Let it speak to you now in the midst of your suffering. "Seldom will there be a more opportune time to share about God than when you are suffering and glorifying Him through it." Now is your chance to discover the profound lessons God can teach you from your own suffering and how you can walk through suffering.

Songs for worship & inspiration this week:

(See Spotify playlist "Glory Chasers")

"For Your Glory" by Tim Timmons "Though you Slay Me" by Shane & Shane

"The Hurt & the Healer" by MercyMe

"For Your Glory & My Good" by All Sons & Daughters

"Glorious Ruins" by Hillsong Worship

"It is Well" by Kristene DiMarco

DAY ONE: HAGAR

Today I invite you into a story that speaks of a woman who endured much pain and suffering. It's a story that serves as a profound example of how God meets us when we feel invisible. It's a story of God providing hope even in the hardest of circumstances. Read Genesis 16. Take note of Hagar's situation.

67. How would you describe her background?

68. What kind of suffering did she endure?

69. Hagar gives God the name "El Roi" in Genesis 16:13, meaning "the God who sees." Why is this such an appropriate name for God?

_____

_____

_____

_____

70. Have you experienced God "seeing you" in the midst of pain or suffering? Write about that time.

_____

_____

_____

_____

Take a moment to share this message of hope with someone today. Write an email, send a text or a card, offer a smile to stranger as a reminder of our "God who sees."

DAY TWO: JOB

The book of Job addresses the question, "Why do godly people suffer?" In many ways, it was an honor that God trusted Job enough to believe he would remain faithful through suffering.

71. Read Job 1. What do you learn about Job's character in Job 1:1-5?

72. Read about Job's first taste of suffering in Job 1:13-22. What was his immediate response to this tragedy? If you have access to the internet, search on YouTube for the video of "Though you Slay Me" by Shane & Shane with words from John Piper. (https://www.youtube.com/watch?v=qyUPz6_TciY) How does this speak to you in your present circumstances?

DAY THREE: JOB

73. The book of Job has universal appeal because all people experience suffering. At many points, Job cries out to God, "Why?" Read Job 3:11-26. Can you relate to Job's heart-cry and questioning?

   _____
   _____
   _____

74. God never gives an explanation to Job for all his suffering, but by the end of the book God makes all things new for Job. Read Job 42:1-6, 10-16. How is faith restored for Job? How did God make things new for Job?

   _____
   _____
   _____

75. How have you seen him take suffering and make things new for you or someone you know?

   _____
   _____
   _____

> **Bonus Glory:**
> "Even though it may seem counterintuitive, it is an honor to suffer. It is a privilege. And we are not to waste it. God wrote suffering into our stories and wants to redeem it for his glory. If we stop shaking our fists at him, we could possibly sit down and see we are running from a life in flames toward a great purpose—one that could never exist without flames."
> —Jennie Allen, *Restless*

DAY FOUR: JESUS

I often have to remind myself that Jesus experienced the agony of suffering. He endured so he could identify with us in our pain. Read Matthew 26:36-46, Mark 14:32-42, Luke 22:39-46—three accounts of what happened in the Garden of Gethsemene.

76. What nuances or differences do you notice in these three different descriptions?

    Matthew

    Mark

    Luke

77. What did the disciples do?

78. What did Jesus do?

79. What would you do?

DAY FIVE: TORN PLACES

80. Ann Voskamp writes in her book, *The Greatest Gift*, "What has torn you, God makes a thin place to see glory."[16] Is there a place where you have been torn this year? Write about it. Make a list. Draw a picture. Craft a poem. Allow yourself to go there, to feel the emotion, to lean into the hard stuff.

81. Write out 1 Peter 1:6-7. Pray for eyes to see glory through that thin or broken place in your story.

DAY SIX: JOURNAL & REFLECT

82. Reflect on your journey this week. Answer one or more of the following questions: How did this week's journey impact you? What did you discover about suffering this week? How can you share His Glory with people who are suffering around you?

_____

_____

_____

_____

_____

_____

_____

_____

_____

_____

_____

Bonus Glory:

"The pupil dilates in the darkness and in the end finds light, just as the soul dilates in misfortune and in the end finds God."

—Victor Hugo, *Les Miserables*

Notes

Glimpses of Glory this Week

WEEK SEVEN
COMMUNITY

When that C-word was spoken over my husband, I was paralyzed by fear of the unknown. I really had no personal experience with cancer. The greatest obstacles for me were not knowing what was ahead and how long we would have to endure. I had never seen my husband really sick or physically broken in our almost-12 years of marriage. He was faithful, strong and fit—my rock in so many ways. I had a sense of security and trust that was suddenly shattered as I tried to digest what the future might hold for him, for me, for our family.

During that time, this very vivid image kept coming back to me. I imagined a gigantic pit in front of me. The sides of the pit were rocky. The pit was dark and deep. I couldn't see the bottom. I couldn't even see how long it extended. I felt my feet up against the sandy, slippery edge of that pit. Everything in me wanted to step back and run the other way, but I felt this strong weight at my back. I had to step forward. I knew my beloved needed me. He was already in the pit. I heard God whispering to me, "It's time to get into the pit." I questioned God. "Why would I want to get in that pit? Can't you just tell me what it looks like? Can't you give me a map of how big and how long and how deep that pit is going to be so I can prepare myself? Couldn't you just heal my man today and we could avoid this pit altogether and point glory back to you?" I heard His gentle voice again, "You need to step into the pit."

I remember the first day I took a step into that pit, expecting to fall headlong into the abyss of the unknown. What I discovered was that God had already lined that pit with people. He had filled that pit with a community of family and friends and strangers. Some of them were people we had invested in over the years. They were church friends, former athletes, students, classmates, neighbors, relatives, former colleagues, people Ericlee had coached at the gym, people we had traveled to Haiti with or who supported the work of our non-profit, friends from our girls' school, and even strangers who were deeply touched by our story.

My foot stepped out but I never hit bottom because there were so many people there to support me. They held my feet strong even when my heart was wavering. They carried me across the pit step by step, day by day. Although the pain was deep, I never really had a sense of touching the bottom. Ever. And now looking back, I wonder: Would I have stepped into the pit if I knew Ericlee would die? Would I have stepped into the pit if God had mapped it out for me? Would I have stepped into the pit if He told me how short or long the journey would be? Probably not. I had to choose to trust, and step forward. I had to believe that all of this was going to be for His glory even though I could not see the full picture.

Through our community, God proved to be "Emmanuel," God with us. In that season of suffering and sickness, I could feel Him right next to me at every turn through the people He provided to journey with me. It was humbling and powerful. It changed me. I learned to receive from others in my brokenness after so many years of giving to others who were broken. I realized God's provision for our family doesn't just mean He gives us health or food or finances. Provision means He has a vision for my future and He is working proactively on my behalf. He doesn't always tell us what the pit looks like because, quite frankly, we couldn't handle it. He simply promises to be with us. He says He will provide a path. And He often provides that path through community.

God's heart beats for community. He Himself embodies community. He is Father, Son and Holy Spirit—three in one—our model of community working seamlessly. He has designed us to live in relationship, to work out our insecurities and use our gifts in the context of authentic community. Living in community is messy and hard but it is also rich with opportunity and a taste of His glory. Emily P. Freeman writes in her book, *A Million Little Ways*, "...we have the capacity to reflect the relational glory of God no matter who we're with, what we're doing, or what's gone wrong."[17] We can try to live independently—islands floating on our own—or we can choose to risk, share our stories and invest in the stories of others.

The Greek word for community is "koinonia," also meaning "fellowship, connection, participation, and partnership."[18] We were built to live in fellowship with one another, to connect and participate in relationships with one another. When we come together, we have the opportunity to challenge and encourage each other. Hebrews 10:24-25 says, "And let us consider how to stir up one another to love and good works, not neglecting to meet together, as is the habit of some, but encouraging one another, and all the more as you see the Day drawing near." (ESV). I love this version because it reminds me that in community we are commanded to continuously gather together for the purpose of caring for one another and inspiring one another. This type of community calls for vulnerability. We have to risk to share our deepest selves. We have to trust others and ask forgiveness when one is wounded.

Our family is a part of a "life group," a collective of five families that meet regularly for meals, prayer, studying the Bible, reading books, celebrating birthdays, and basically doing life together. We have been meeting together for more than 10 years. We started out all attending the same church but different families have different needs and now we all participate in different faith communities. We haven't given up meeting. When we get together, it always involves good food, a gaggle of kids (17 among us) and a whole lot of laughter.

There are certainly tears too. We have walked through many challenging seasons together, including infertility, strains in marriage, losing jobs, moving, financial trouble, births, adoption of children, supporting aging parents, the death of a baby and more. These are friends who have become family. The weekend we learned of Ericlee's cancer diagnosis, those friends came to our house and gathered in our messy bedroom and prayed. We all got down on our faces together and cried out to God for healing. I prayed a reckless, wild prayer and confessed all my fears in front of those friends. We surrendered the future together.

When people come together in community, we have the ability to bear each other's burdens as it says in Galatians 6:2, and lighten each other's load. There's a Honduran proverb that says, "Grief shared is half grief; Joy shared is double joy." When my husband died, the power of this proverb came to life for me. Many people joined me in my grief. They entered into the painful places, the memories with me. This did not take away the grief, but it made it somehow more bearable. As humans, our nature is to avoid pain. Sometimes grief is about returning to the places where you laid your most precious memories and remembering, and then finding the grace and strength to forge new memories. It's about wading through instead of marching around. Walking this grief journey with my people has somehow given me more courage than if I were to walk it alone.

I remember the first time I went running with my friends after my husband's death. Running had always been a place of connection for us. Throughout our marriage, we made a host of memories and built community through running. We ran more 10ks, half marathons, and marathons together than I could count. We coached high school track and field together for 9 years. We trained teams of people to run half marathons while getting fit and raising money for Haiti. I knew running was something I had to redeem for myself after losing Ericlee. I knew it would be hard. I knew it could be part of the path to healing.

That first night a group of us met at a local high school track, where we had coached many of our teams. I walked out across those lanes under the lights, and I felt Ericlee there. I started my workout and his coaching voice echoed around every curve. I hadn't run for months. The air burned in my lungs and my legs felt heavy, but I ran. I ran, and I ran. And on the last lap, I cried. Drenched in sweat and tears, I wondered how I could ever keep running without him by my side. In that moment, I turned and realized I was surrounded by a great cloud of witnesses as it talks about in Hebrews 12:1. They too heard his coaching voice on the track. My friends gathered around me and we cried together and soon the tears gave way to laughter.

Through community we can be Emmanuel (God with us) to others. We can share His glory story around the table. We can offer our presence and our resources to those in need. We can stand by that friend facing divorce or grieving a miscarriage or the death of a loved one.

When we build trust, when we risk vulnerability, when we extend grace, we also uncover freedom and glory. The book of 1 John was written by John, the beloved disciple and friend of Jesus. The prologue to this book unfolds what John found to be true through his time with Jesus.

John speaks simply about the glory story he experienced. I John 1:3-4 says, "We saw it, we heard it, and now we're telling you so you can experience it along with us, this experience of communion with the Father and his Son, Jesus Christ. Our motive for writing is simply this: We want you to enjoy this, too. Your joy will double our joy!" (The Message).

These verses are reminiscent of that Honduran proverb. They remind me that when I enter into authentic community with people and with Christ, my grief is halved; my joy is multiplied. The real C-word God created to reflect His glory and grace is community. This week, I invite you to discover how God is with us daily through our community.

Songs for worship & inspiration this week:

(see Spotify playlist "Glory Chasers")

"No Man is an Island" by Tenth Avenue North
"Broken Together" by Casting Crowns
"Whole Again (Come Alive)" by Lincoln Brewster
"You Amaze Us" by Selah
"With Everything" by Hillsong Worship

> **Memory Verse:**
> "Let us think of ways to motivate one another to acts of love and good works. And let us not neglect our meeting together, as some people do, but encourage one another, especially now that the day of his return is drawing near."
> –Hebrews 10:24-25 (NLT)

DAY ONE: CHURCH OF ACTS

83. Read Acts 2:41-47. What do you think these verses are saying about living in community?

_____

_____

_____

_____

84. How did the people of the church in the book of Acts care for one another?

_____

_____

_____

_____

85. How would you describe their attitudes toward others in their community?

86. What can you learn from this snapshot of the early church?

> **Bonus Glory:**
> "Because there really is nothing like good friends, like the sounds of their laughter and the tones of their voices and the things they teach us in the quietest, smallest moments."
> —Shauna Niequist, *Bittersweet*

DAY TWO: MY COMMUNITY

87. I challenge you this week to write a story about your community. Think about a group, a team, a tribe, a family, a collective of people you have been a part of and how that experience of community has changed you. Who was there? Where did you gather? What united you? What was messy? What made it worth it? What did you learn about yourself and God and others? I'm asking you to join me as co-writers today. It doesn't have to be perfect or polished or poetry. Just write your story.

DAY THREE: PROVERBS

The book of Proverbs was written primarily by King Solomon. He asked God for a discerning heart to help govern God's people. Proverbs is designed to help us make wise choices and live in community with one another. Read Proverbs 27:17 in 3 or 4 different versions of the Bible.

88. Write out one version in the space below.

_____

_____

_____

_____

89. What is the wisdom in this proverb?

_____

_____

_____

_____

90. Do you have someone in your life who sharpens you? How did you meet or how did they come into your life?

_____

_____

_____

DAY FOUR: DYNAMIC DUOS

Annie F. Downs writes in her book, *Let's All Be Brave*, about how her community gave her courage: "I think that's what I need most to be brave—a place where I belong. And you only find that place when you find those people... No one is brave alone. Every superhero has someone they come home to; every Bible character has someone they depend on. Jesus has his disciples and his family. Batman had Robin. Paul had Barnabas. Ruth had Naomi. The Incredibles had each other; Superman had Lois Lane. Moses had Aaron, Hur, and Miriam. Noah had his family. So we see modeled, even in the Bible, the truth that the bravest among us do not stand alone."[19]

91. Take some time to look up a couple of the stories of these pairs or groups. How did they depend on each other? How did they strengthen and sharpen each other? How did they give each other courage?

    Jesus & His disciples [See Matthew 4:18-22]

    _____

    _____

    Batman & Robin

    _____

    _____

    Paul & Barnabas [See Acts 13]

    _____

    _____

Ruth & Naomi [See Ruth 1:1-19]

_____

_____

The Incredibles

_____

_____

Superman & Lois Lane

_____

_____

Moses & Aaron, Hur & Miriam [See Exodus 17:10-13]

_____

_____

Noah & his family [See Genesis 7:1]

_____

_____

92. Have you ever had a person or group of friends infuse you with courage like Annie's quote and these examples?

DAY FIVE: JESUS PRAYS

93. Jesus prays for all believers in John 17: 20-25. Read this passage. Circle the word "glory" used in His prayer. Underline any repeated words.

1 "I do not ask for these only, but also for those who will believe in me through their word,

2 that they may all be one, just as you, Father, are in me, and I in you, that they also may be in us, so that the world may believe that you have sent me.

3 The glory that you have given me I have given to them, that they may be one even as we are one,

4 I in them and you in me, that they may become perfectly one, so that the world may know that you sent me and loved them even as you loved me.

5 Father, I desire that they also, whom you have given me, may be with me where I am, to see my glory that you have given me because you loved me before the foundation of the world.

6 O righteous Father, even though the world does not know you, I know you, and these know that you have sent me.

7 I made known to them your name, and I will continue to make it known, that the love with which you have loved me may be in them, and I in them." (ESV)

COMMUNITY

94. This passage is a prayer from Jesus to the Father. What is Jesus asking for in this prayer?

_____

_____

_____

_____

_____

95. In verses 22-24, Jesus talks about believers entering into community with God through a shared glory. What does that mean to you?

_____

_____

_____

_____

_____

DAY SIX: JOURNAL & REFLECT

96. Reflect on your journey this week. Answer one or more of the following questions: What did you discover about community this week? In what ways will you chase His glory through your circles of friends, neighbors and community? How can you share His glory with people who might not have a strong community of support?

Notes

GLORY CHASERS

Glimpses of Glory this Week

WEEK EIGHT
JUSTICE

I remember the sticky vinyl seats of the big yellow school bus. I remember the sun blaring down, exposing shiny metals and swirling colors. I remember driving past mountains upon mountains of garbage. More than anything I remember the stench. As our bus labored through the gate, the smell was so putrid that we all had to hold our breath. We were entering the largest garbage dump in Latin America and one of the largest in the world. I was with a collective of Christian college students from all over the United States. We had no idea what we would encounter on this field trip of sorts. The memory of that place is seared in my heart forever.

In the next several hours, we came face to face with the most extreme poverty I had ever witnessed. More than 11,000 people live and work near that dump in the heart of Guatemala City, and 6,500 of them are children. Many of these human beings are scavengers, who spend their days scouring the garbage for food and anything they might recycle or sell to survive. Children play in the rubble. Adults and children sniff glue to avoid the overwhelming stench of the dump and to escape from their existence.

We pulled up next to The Potter's House, a place of ministry in the heart of this dump. In that place of refuge, we met men, women and children who had hearts to turn trash into treasure. One courageous woman had followed a vision that eventually became a non-profit organization to bring respect and dignity to those who were treated as little better than the trash where they found their existence. I heard stories of young people who were cultivating a personal relationship with Jesus Christ and now getting their education as a result of the Potter's House. I saw faith in action right there in the rubble.

As we drove away from the dump that day, many of my classmates started taking pictures through the windows of our bus. I stood to join them. I thought it was a good idea to remember this day, this place, this moment. I tried to focus through the lens of my camera. My eyes froze on a little girl digging through the garbage. I experienced something I had never experienced before—a righteous anger. I actually hurled my camera at the back of the bus. I was so angry and equally sad and frustrated that this little girl had to live in such overwhelming filth. I wondered how this kind of poverty could exist when so many lived in luxury in the place I called home. I slumped into my seat and sobbed.

I would say this experience was a critical junction in my justice journey. I already had a heart for social justice issues as I was raised by a mother who is passionate about issues like civil rights and racial equality. When I was teased or bullied as a child for being a brown girl in a predominantly white neighborhood, she was the one talking me through. She was the one helping me write honor society essays about the value of multiculturalism and Voice of America speeches about equality. She had encouraged my heart of compassion in high school for children, especially orphans.

That day in Guatemala City I came face to face with another issue of justice that began to stitch its way deeply into my soul. God was growing in me a heart for the poor and marginalized. He would continue to cultivate that heart, and years later it would lead to signing up for a mission trip to Haiti with the young singles group from my church.

From the moment I disembarked from that little prop plane, Haiti and its people captured my heart. After that first journey to Pignon, Haiti, I felt the tug on my heart to return. I quit my job in Fresno, California, and moved to Haiti to teach English. Through Haiti, I met my husband Ericlee, who was the grandson of pioneer missionaries in the country. After we were married we pursued justice work together directing a non-profit in Haiti that reached across the northern mountains.

The word "justice" conjures up a diversity of images and meanings for different people. I believe it's also an integral part of the heart of God and how we can participate in His glory story. The work of bringing about justice is always multi-layered and complex. In a secular context, justice is about getting what you deserve. The dictionary defines justice as "administering of deserved punishment or reward"[20] and connects it with righteousness, moral conduct, equitableness. Of course, this definition is devoid of an important ingredient—faith. I prefer Julie Clawson's definition in her book, *Everyday Justice: The Global Impact of our Daily Choices*: "Justice is to represent God's love to each other and thereby honor the image of God in the other person as well."[21] Her definition helps articulate the difference between punitive justice (getting what you deserve) and restorative justice (giving what will restore someone to understanding they are an image bearer of God).

I believe we are called to be a part of restorative justice in the world. As image bearers of God, we can participate in setting things right in the world so others can live fully in their purpose as image bearers of God. I love the way Pastor Mitchel Lee unpacks this in his sermon, "Brave Faith: Justice and the Mission of God." One of his main points is that restorative justice is relational. Jesus came to earth to restore relationships. As disciples of Christ, we need to follow his leading. Lee points us to the capstone story in Luke 4:16-21 when Jesus comes into the synagogue in Nazareth, where he was brought up, and strategically reads from the scroll of the prophet of Isaiah (see Isaiah 61). "As usual, he entered the synagogue on the Sabbath day and stood up to read. The scroll of the prophet Isaiah was given to Him, and unrolling the scroll. He found the place where it was written: 'The Spirit of the Lord is on Me, because He has anointed Me to preach good news to the poor. He has sent Me to proclaim freedom to the captives and recovery of sight to the blind, to set free the oppressed, to proclaim the year of the Lord's favor.' He then rolled up the scroll, gave it back to the attendant, and sat down. And the eyes of everyone in the synagogue were fixed on Him. He began by saying to them, 'Today as you listen, this Scripture has been fulfilled'" (HCSB). I am struck by two things in this passage: First, this is Jesus' mission statement. Second, Jesus is not just reading this prophecy. He's boldly telling all those listening that he is the fulfillment of this prophecy. It's significant that Jesus points to the importance of justice work here. He highlights that one of his main purposes in coming to earth is to set things right for the poor, the captives, the blind, and the oppressed for the Glory of God. Jesus' entire ministry on earth models justice work for us.[22]

Biblical justice is not an isolated cause or a project to support. It should be part of our life mission when we become Christians. Ken Wytsma writes in *Pursuing Justice: The Call to Live and Die For Bigger Things*, "If we ignore justice, like ignoring love or truth, we create a caricature rather than the divine character we meet in Scripture and in our lives. Justice is a hallmark of God, a distinctive and pure feature of His character that defines Him and His will for the world."[23] Wytsma underscores this idea again that justice is part of God's character, His heart, His image, and as image bearers we have a call to reflect His glory through doing justice work. When we seize opportunities to give our lives away on behalf of others, we participate in and reflect His glory.

What does this mean in practical terms? James 1:27 says it this way: "Pure and undefiled religion before our God and Father is this: to look after orphans and widows in their distress and to keep oneself unstained by the world." According to the Holman Christian Standard Version Study Bible for Women, orphans and widows were considered the most vulnerable in James' society. They needed protection and provision.[24] James calls Jewish Christians in his time and all of us today to action. He articulates this as "undefiled religion"—a way to practice and live out our faith.

I love the concept of synergy. It's the idea that when two or more elements are combined they can produce something greater than the sum of those elements. This applies to people too. We are more powerful to fight injustice together. R. York Moore writes in his book, *Making All Things New: God's Dream for Global Justice*, "The dream of God includes us—our efforts, our passions and our risks—to establish his dream where it is not. The dream of God is not merely a future reality. It is a reality that we can taste, touch, feel and live today if only we reach for it together."[25] When we engage in the hard work of justice side by side, we can embody God's glory here on earth.

This week I am calling each one of you to start thinking about ways you can chase His glory by participating in justice work in our world. When we speak up on behalf of our brothers and sisters, when we offer a dose of grace to a family member, when we serve the least of these, when we lay down our earthly treasures so others can live in their worth as treasure of the Most High King, we experience His glory again. Pursuing justice demonstrates love to others and brings an offering to God. It's a way to honor His Creation, to enter His Presence, to worship Him in our daily lives, to bring Him fame, to identify with His suffering, and to discover rich community.

Songs for worship & inspiration this week:

(see Spotify playlist "Glory Chasers")

"Hands and Feet" by The Brilliance
"Mighty to Save" by Shane & Shane
"Daisy's Song" by Dominic Balli
"Open Up" by The Brilliance
"The Glory of it All" by David Crowder
"Human Race" by Jars of Clay
"The Power of your Name" by Lincoln Brewster

> **Memory Verse:**
> *"He has told you, O man, what is good; and what does the LORD require of you but to do justice, and to love kindness, and to walk humbly with your God?"*
> —Micah 6:8 (ESV)

DAY ONE: ISAIAH

God's heart for Justice is especially prominent in the book of Isaiah. According to Ray Stedman's commentary, Isaiah's prophecy is the fullest revelation of Christ to be found in the Old Testament. Isaiah reveals God's heart and plan for salvation through His coming son. Stedman writes, "Isaiah saw how God's love would break the back of humanity's rebelliousness, and, despite our stubborn perversity, would open a way of restoration. Then at last, beyond the darkness of centuries yet to come, there would be a morning without clouds, the Day of Righteousness, when God's glory would fill the earth, and people would make war no more".[28]

97. Look up the following verses. What do you think each of these passages is saying about justice. Note how justice and righteousness often go hand in hand in God's economy.

    Isaiah 1:26-27

    _____

    _____

    _____

    Isaiah 5:7

    _____

    _____

    _____

Isaiah 5:16

Isaiah 28:17

Isaiah 30:18

Isaiah 42:1-4

98. After reading these passages, how do you think justice is a part of God's bigger glory story?

DAY TWO: ISAIAH 61

As described in the Introduction on Justice, Isaiah 61 is the mission and the prophecy Jesus came to fulfill.

99. Read Isaiah 61 on the next page. Underline any words or phrases that you think hold important meaning.

Isaiah 61 New International Version (NIV)   The Year of the LORD's Favor

> 61 The Spirit of the Sovereign LORD is on me,
>   because the LORD has anointed me
>   to proclaim good news to the poor.
> He has sent me to bind up the brokenhearted,
>   to proclaim freedom for the captives
>   and release from darkness for the prisoners,
> 2 to proclaim the year of the LORD's favor
>   and the day of vengeance of our God,
>   to comfort all who mourn,
> 3 and provide for those who grieve in Zion—
>   to bestow on them a crown of beauty
>   instead of ashes,
>   the oil of joy
>   instead of mourning,
>   and a garment of praise
>   instead of a spirit of despair.
> They will be called oaks of righteousness,
>   a planting of the LORD
>   for the display of his splendor.
> 4 They will rebuild the ancient ruins
>   and restore the places long devastated;
>   they will renew the ruined cities
>   that have been devastated for generations.
> 5 Strangers will shepherd your flocks;
>   foreigners will work your fields and vineyards.

6 *And you will be called priests of the LORD,*
  you will be named ministers of our God.
    You will feed on the wealth of nations,
    and in their riches you will boast.
7 *Instead of your shame*
    you will receive a double portion,
  and instead of disgrace
    you will rejoice in your inheritance.
  And so you will inherit a double portion in your land,
    and everlasting joy will be yours.
8 *"For I, the LORD, love justice;*
    I hate robbery and wrongdoing.
  In my faithfulness I will reward my people
    and make an everlasting covenant with them.
9 *Their descendants will be known among the nations*
    and their offspring among the peoples.
  All who see them will acknowledge
    that they are a people the LORD has blessed."
10 *I delight greatly in the LORD;*
    my soul rejoices in my God.
  For he has clothed me with garments of salvation
    and arrayed me in a robe of his righteousness,
  as a bridegroom adorns his head like a priest,
    and as a bride adorns herself with her jewels.
11 *For as the soil makes the sprout come up*
    and a garden causes seeds to grow,
  so the Sovereign LORD will make righteousness
    and praise spring up before all nations.

100. What is the main point or thesis of this chapter?

101. What do you learn about God's heart for justice through this chapter? How does justice intersect with God's glory in this prophecy?

DAY THREE: MICAH 6

Micah was a prophet from a small town in Judah. He prophesied in a time of great political upheaval. His poetic prophesies start with a call to listen, a judgment from God, and often conclude with a message of encouragement and hope.

102. Read Micah 6:1-16. What is the nature of the questions presented in verses 6-7?

103. In Micah 6:8, God reveals 3 things He requires of his people. What are they?

104. Refer back to the introduction from this week. What is the difference between punitive and restorative justice?

105. What type of justice do you think Micah 6:8 highlights?

106. What are some practical ways you can live out these verses?

DAY FOUR: RUTH

This week we are diving into the book of Ruth in the Bible. If you have never read this book before, I recommend listening to it through the YouVersion Bible app or reading it in a children's Bible. This book is only four chapters long but it is packed with tragedy, love, justice and redemption. As you listen or read, think about how God's glory shines through the story.

107. What kind of tragedy and suffering did Ruth & Naomi endure? (See 1:1-6)

108. How would you describe Ruth's character? (See 1:14-17)

109. How does Boaz find out about Ruth's character? (See 2:5-12; 3:10-11)

110. What kind of man is Boaz? (See 2:1)

111. How is Boaz careful to offer Ruth a sense of dignity even as he provides for her needs? (See 2:8-17)

112. Explain your understanding of the "kinsman-redeemer" role that Boaz accepts. (See 2:20-4:12)

113. Boaz participates in a kind of justice work that redeems both Ruth and her mother-in-law Naomi as well as his own life. What can you learn about justice and God's glory through their story?

DAY FIVE: JUSTICE WORK

There are certain things that prick our hearts, which make us well up or weep. In that place we can often find our passion and our purpose in justice work. Ken Wytsma writes, "If we don't cry, we shouldn't sing. The connection between lament and justice is an oft-neglected relationship. Engagement in justice and our worship and knowledge of God are inextricable"[29]

114. Make a list of all the injustices you see around you and in the world. Go back and circle the ones that make you cry or tug on your heart strings. Maybe it's the number of starving children around the world or sex trafficking or racism or the plight of orphans or the broken prison system. Maybe it's the widow, the divorcee, the alcoholic, the refugee, the anorexic, the homeless. Write about that passion.

_____

_____

_____

_____

115. If you can't think of one, give yourself permission to go down a rabbit trail. Research a project in your city or an organization doing justice work in the world. Share what you learned.

_____

_____

_____

Bonus Glory:

"If God's character includes a zeal for justice that leads him to have the tenderest love and closest involvement with the socially weak, then what shall God's people be like? They must be people who are likewise passionately concerned for the weak and vulnerable."

—Timothy Keller, *Generous Justice*

DAY SIX: JOURNAL & REFLECT

116. Reflect on your journey this week. Answer one or more of the following questions: What did you discover about justice this week that you didn't know before? How did this week's journey impact you? In what ways will you chase His glory in pursuing justice in your community and our world?

Notes

Glimpses of Glory this Week

WEEK NINE
HEAVEN

His breathing changed, tightened, quickened. Each breath was a labor. I had a hard time believing this sound was coming from my beloved. After almost 12 years of listening to the cadence of his breath as we trained and ran marathons together, as he slept by my side, this sound was so foreign. When you get to really know someone, when you live with them and enter their personal space, you know how they breathe. His gasping for air was painful to my heart. I could visibly see the bumps across his chest—the cancer had spread throughout his lungs. I tried to hook up the oxygen tank brought by hospice care. Twice I connected the tubes to his nostrils. Twice he ripped them out. He was still fighting.

His mom was there with me. She told me with her eyes that we were near the end. One by one I ushered my daughters into the room and urged them to kiss daddy one more time. When our two-year-old bounded onto the bed, he lifted his eyes. His breathing calmed for a few split seconds. She brought him that one last glimmer, but then his breathing returned to that strange, laboring sound. We went on for a few more hours. I cradled his hand in mine. His mom held his other hand. My parents sat at the foot of the bed, my mom singing, "Come to Jesus." I choke-whispered the words—still in denial that my beloved was standing on the threshold of Heaven. "And with your final heartbeat/kiss the world goodbye/ Then go in peace, and laugh on Glory's side/ and Fly to Jesus."[28] Then came dawn. Light streamed wildly through the blinds of our bedroom window.

His hazel eyes moved—following, seeking, searching. We all saw it. His eyes had been flat and distant for hours, but suddenly they were alive and drawn to that window. His eyes saw something we could not see. He clapped his hands together. Leaving his broken body behind, he leaped into Glory.

My younger brother, who is not a writer, penned a beautiful vision of my beloved entering into Heaven after months of enduring such pain and suffering. Here is an excerpt:

> *"As he approached, the officials grabbed another ribbon and stretched it across the finish line. We held our breath anticipating his grand completion. With the last ounce of energy and the last breath of air, he stretched out his arms in victory...To this father, son, brother, coach, missionary, and friend: How could he know that I loved him, and I was proud of him, and I would never forget him? Then I see him. He is lit up. At the top of the hill, past the finish line, and high above the crowd, he is standing strong and tall. His body is restored, and he is looking back at us. There is a smile on his face as he claps his hands together and waves goodbye. His eyes are gleaming and his face bright. There is no need for words. He turns towards the light and continues on."*

I love this vision of my beloved because it is a picture of glory. It is a snapshot in my mind of him following the light and being glorified with Christ. Ericlee lived every moment of his life to give God glory. He chose heaven. And I believe he is enjoying all the treasures heaven has to offer today. I grieve the loss of him, but I grieve with the hope of heaven. 1 Thessalonians 4:13, says "...we want you to know what will happen to the believers who have died so you will not grieve like people who have no hope" (NLT).

I have hope that I will see Ericlee again someday when I graduate to heaven too. I have thought about heaven more in the last year than I ever have in my whole lifetime. I have read books. I have searched verses in the Bible. I have talked about it at the dinner table with my girls.

Together we imagine what Daddy might be doing in heaven. I think of him sitting at a grand campfire, unfolding stories with his grandparents, or asking his faith heroes Abraham and Noah questions, or meeting his favorite missionary-runner Eric Liddell. The girls tell me they think Daddy is leading a CrossFit class for angels. Sometimes we imagine him running marathons on golden streets or eating his favorite cookies and cream ice cream to his heart's content. Most of all, I am guessing my beloved is tracing glory. He is looking out and seeing all the threads of his life with a heavenly perspective—all glory. He understands the nuances of all I can't even fathom today.

Throughout this study, we have unpacked various meanings for the word glory. We talked about how God's glory is reflected in creation and how the God-Artist created us to create. We entered into His Presence by chasing glory moments with our families, in nature and through the stories of several Bible figures. We learned to worship Him in new ways, looking for new avenues to purpose our posture to bring Him glory. We wrestled with notions of fame and how we are called to make God famous through telling His glory story. We contemplated the weight of glory for Jesus Christ through suffering and how we join him as we taste suffering. We explored the idea that community opens doors for us to participate in and share His glory with others. We even grappled with the idea that justice is the heart of God and the place we are called to administer grace and glory in our world.

The culminating definition of the word "glory" is synonymous with the word "heaven." We talk about going to Glory one day or meeting Christ in Glory. Many of the old hymns talk about mansions in Glory and going home to Glory. The glory referred to here is the Glory of heaven.

We sing about heaven as the ultimate glory, but do we really believe in it? Do we imagine heaven as a wonderful place? Are we fixing our eyes on our eternal future with hope or reluctantly offering it as an alternative to the fiery hell?

> **Memory Verse:**
>
> *Set your minds on things that are above, not on things that are on earth. For you have died, and your life is hidden with Christ in God. When Christ who is your life appears, then you also will appear with him in glory.*
> —Colossians 3:2-4

Randy Alcorn points out in his comprehensive book, *Heaven*, "As human beings we have a terminal disease called mortality. The current death rate is 100 percent. Unless Christ returns soon, we're all going to die. We don't like to think about death; yet, worldwide, 3 people die every second, 180 every minute, and nearly 11,000 every hour. If the Bible is right about what happens to us after death, it means that more than 250,000 people every day go either to Heaven or Hell."[29] Yet, Heaven remains elusive to many believers. We don't take time to learn about Heaven, talk about it, or dream about what it might be like. I've certainly heard more sermons about hell in my lifetime than I have about heaven. I long to know more.

We have to choose heaven. Romans 3:23 reminds us "all have sinned and fall short of the glory of God" (ESV). If we choose to believe in Jesus Christ as our Savior, we are invited to join Him in Heaven to taste that ultimate glory of God referenced in Romans. The Bible actually gives us lots of pictures of Heaven if we go digging. This week I'm going to have you do just that. I'm going to have you search the scriptures and imagine with me what the ultimate Glory might be like. As we learn and dream, I believe we will be filled with a longing to pursue His glory and holiness.

I love the way Alcorn frames it, "Heaven should affect our activities and ambitions, our recreation and friendships, and the way we spend our money and time. If I believe I'll spend eternity in a world of unending beauty and adventure, will I be content to spend all my evenings staring at game shows, sitcoms, and ball games?... What will last forever? God's Word. People. Spending time in God's Word and investing in people will pay off in eternity and bring me joy and perspective now."[30] I know the death of my Ericlee has pushed me to reconsider Heaven and restructure my life here on earth. I want to chase God's glory in every moment, in every opportunity, in every sunset, in every relationship.

Songs for worship & inspiration this week:

(see Spotify playlist "Glory Chasers")

"I See Heaven" by Bryan & Katie Torwalt
"When the Saints" by Sara Groves
"Let the Heavens Open" by Kari Jobe
"I See the Lord" by WOW, Chris Falson
"Into the Glorious" by Christy Nockels
"Untitled Hymn (Come to Jesus)" by Chris Rice

DAY ONE: RESURRECTION

In Colossians 3:1-4, Paul urges us to seek the things above. Earlier in this letter Paul talks about identifying with Christ through his suffering and death. Here he turns to identifying with Christ through his resurrection to Heaven. Read Colossians 3:1-4.

117. What is significant about being seated at the right hand of God?

118. What do you think are the "things above" Paul refers to in verse 2?

119. How will we share in Christ's glory mentioned in verse 4?

120. Read Matthew 6:33. How does this verse complement the passage from Colossians 3?

121. How is "seeking" an ongoing process, not a one-time thought or conversation? What does it look like in your life?

DAY TWO: LIFE IN HEAVEN

When it comes to heaven, we are often filled with questions. Randy Alcorn tries to unpack some of these questions in his book, Heaven. I urge you to go on your own treasure hunt through the scriptures for answers to some of these common questions about heaven. Feel free to read the suggested passages and then find your own that relate. Jot down what you learn.

122. Read John 14:1-4. Where will we live?

_____

_____

_____

123. Read Revelation 6:10 and Luke 6:21. Will we have emotions?

_____

_____

_____

124. Read Job 19:26 and Philippians 3:20-21. Will we have bodies in heaven?

_____

_____

_____

125. What other questions do you have about heaven?

_____

_____

DAY THREE: DREAMING OF HEAVEN

A popular song played or sung at funerals is "I Can Only Imagine" by Mercy Me. This song opens the door for all of us to imagine what it might be like to meet Jesus face to face one day surrounded by Glory.[31]

126. How do you imagine heaven? What do you imagine you will do when you meet Jesus?

_____

_____

_____

_____

127. Think about a friend or relative who you believe is in heaven today. What do you imagine that person doing? How might they be experiencing glory and redemption from their life on earth?

_____

_____

_____

_____

128. Write a poem or song about heaven incorporating some of what you have learned this week.

DAY FOUR: THE NEW EARTH

We can live with a hope of heaven, where many family members and friends exist now, but we also have the hope of the new earth. There are many descriptions of the new earth and new jerusalem throughout scripture. Look up the following verses. What do you learn from the following verses?

129. Job 19:25-27

130. Psalm 102:15-17

131. Isaiah 40:9-11

_____

_____

_____

132. Haggai 2:6-7

_____

_____

_____

DAY FIVE: THE NEW JERUSALEM

133. Read through Revelation 21 below. This chapter gives the most comprehensive and detailed picture of the new heaven and new earth. Make a list or draw a picture of some of the key parts of this place.

> 1 Then I saw "a new heaven and a new earth," for the first heaven and the first earth had passed away, and there was no longer any sea.
>
> 2 I saw the Holy City, the new Jerusalem, coming down out of heaven from God, prepared as a bride beautifully dressed for her husband.
>
> 3 And I heard a loud voice from the throne saying, "Look! God's dwelling place is now among the people, and he will dwell with them. They will be his people, and God himself will be with them and be their God.
>
> 4 "He will wipe every tear from their eyes. There will be no more death or mourning or crying or pain, for the old order of things has passed away."

5   He who was seated on the throne said, "I am making everything new!" Then he said, "Write this down, for these words are trustworthy and true."

6   He said to me: "It is done. I am the Alpha and the Omega, the Beginning and the End. To the thirsty I will give water without cost from the spring of the water of life.

7   Those who are victorious will inherit all this, and I will be their God and they will be my children.

8   But the cowardly, the unbelieving, the vile, the murderers, the sexually immoral, those who practice magic arts, the idolaters and all liars—they will be consigned to the fiery lake of burning sulfur. This is the second death."

9   One of the seven angels who had the seven bowls full of the seven last plagues came and said to me, "Come, I will show you the bride, the wife of the Lamb."

10 And he carried me away in the Spirit to a mountain great and high, and showed me the Holy City, Jerusalem, coming down out of heaven from God.

11 It shone with the glory of God, and its brilliance was like that of a very precious jewel, like a jasper, clear as crystal

12 It had a great, high wall with twelve gates, and with twelve angels at the gates. On the gates were written the names of the twelve tribes of Israel.

13 There were three gates on the east, three on the north, three on the south and three on the west.

14 The wall of the city had twelve foundations, and on them were the names of the twelve apostles of the Lamb.

15 The angel who talked with me had a measuring rod of gold to measure the city, its gates and its walls.

16 The city was laid out like a square, as long as it was wide. He measured the city with the rod and found it to be 12,000 stadia in length, and as wide and high as it is long.

17 The angel measured the wall using human measurement, and it was 144 cubits thick.

18 The wall was made of jasper, and the city of pure gold, as pure as glass.

19 The foundations of the city walls were decorated with every kind of precious stone. The first foundation was jasper, the second sapphire, the third agate, the fourth emerald,

20 the fifth onyx, the sixth ruby, the seventh chrysolite, the eighth beryl, the ninth topaz, the tenth turquoise, the eleventh jacinth, and the twelfth amethyst.

21 The twelve gates were twelve pearls, each gate made of a single pearl. The great street of the city was of gold, as pure as transparent glass.

22 I did not see a temple in the city, because the Lord God Almighty and the Lamb are its temple.

23 The city does not need the sun or the moon to shine on it, for the glory of God gives it light, and the Lamb is its lamp.

24 The nations will walk by its light, and the kings of the earth will bring their splendor into it.

25 On no day will its gates ever be shut, for there will be no night there.

26 The glory and honor of the nations will be brought into it.

27 Nothing impure will ever enter it, nor will anyone who does what is shameful or deceitful, but only those whose names are written in the Lamb's book of life.

134. How does this new heaven and new earth reflect His ultimate glory?

DAY SIX: JOURNAL & REFLECT

Reflect on your journey this week. What made the biggest impact on you? In what ways will you look to Glory in Heaven in the days to come? How can you encourage others with the Hope of Heaven?

_____

_____

_____

_____

_____

_____

_____

_____

_____

_____

_____

_____

_____

> **Bonus Glory:**
>
> *"What delivers us from the fear of death? What takes away death's sting? Only a relationship with the person who died on our behalf, the one who has gone ahead to make a place for us to live with him. If we don't know Jesus, we will fear death and its sting—and we should."*
>
> —Randy Alcorn, *Heaven*

Notes

Glimpses of Glory this Week

WEEK TEN
CLOSING THOUGHTS: BEAUTY FROM ASHES

The airlines had allowed us to change our tickets from the previous May when we were scheduled to travel to Haiti. By then, the cancer was already spreading through his body. He urged me to go without him but I couldn't bear the thought of boarding that plane with the uncertainty of leaving him sick at home. I'm so glad I stayed. Yet, my heart grieved all that summer that we could not return to our second home, our mission, our Haiti. It was a secondary loss for me. Not only was I losing my husband, I was also losing my life mission. Haiti was the place I found my sweet spot, the place I felt most alive in my skin, the place I had come to understand God's calling on my life. Haiti was a hard place—full of adversity and strife, poverty and politics—and yet, it was calling me still.

I jumped through the proverbial hoops to get our tickets changed to the new date—nine months after our original scheduled date to depart. I had to write a letter explaining our situation, including a copy of his death certificate. Several weeks went by and then I received an email that they would honor our tickets. I worked with an agent on the phone to book the flights. When I received the itinerary, I put it aside. I somehow compartmentalized the trip and all it entailed to an empty part of the back of my mind.

Bonus Glory:

"I believe the glory of God is the going public of his infinite worth. I define the holiness of God as the infinite value of God, the infinite intrinsic worth of God. And when that goes public in creation, the heavens are telling the glory of God, and human beings are manifesting his glory, because we're created in his image, and we're trusting his promises so that we make him look gloriously trustworthy."

—John Piper, *"What is God's glory?"*

> **Bonus Glory:**
> *The Word became flesh and moved into the neighborhood. We saw the glory with our own eyes, the one-of-a-kind glory, like Father, like Son, Generous inside and out, true from start to finish.*
> —John 1:14 (MSG)

As the trip grew closer, I felt anxiety rising up inside of me until one day it broke like a dam releasing water. The tears, the emotions, the fear all mingled and rushed out in a flood of tears. Could I really do this? Could I travel across the country with three little girls in tow without him? Could I go back to the place where we had fallen in love? Could I face the memories? Could I find a new place in Haiti now in this new context? Everything in me that felt torn and broken was magnified through the lens of this trip. What in the world had I gotten myself into? Where was the glory in all of this? I did not realize until later that the weight of this trip would be in the heart work I had to do before departure. I had to lean into the hard. I had to find the courage Ericlee had modeled for me all these years. I needed to allow the prayers of my friends and family to cover me. I needed to give myself grace and choose faith over my fears.

Two weeks later, I walked through our old farm house in the Northern mountains of Haiti. The familiar smell of sautéed garlic, fragrant cloves and Haitian-fried chicken wafted to my nose. I passed the raw wood dining table he had built with our friends with enough seats for a team of 16-20 people. I continued down the hall past the room where I had first stayed when I lived in Haiti on my own almost a decade earlier. That trip was for the purpose of teaching English to some of the leaders. The trip where God started to write a new story in my broken heart. That was the room where (much to my chagrin) the mice ran free and the spiders spun their webs above my head. That was the room where I had laid many days sick in bed, reading novels and crying out to God in my loneliness. My soul was somehow home.

My eyes rested on the mirror hanging crooked on the wall in the tropical green hallway. We had received that mirror with our names etched across it as a wedding gift. We had no idea where to put it in our California home so we had brought it to Haiti. I plopped down my carry-on bag in our bedroom—the second one on the right with that generations-old dresser and the homemade double bed. My mind mulled over the countless summer nights we had packed our family of five into this small room. I remembered the stifling heat that felt heavy like a weighted blanket and mosquitoes buzzing incessantly in our ears. I remembered the way he would turn off the generator and check the doors so vigilantly each night. Everything about this house whispered memories to me.

I pushed through the back screen door and walked out into the night. A canopy of stars spread overhead and an almost-full moon illuminated the indigo sky. I stepped through the gate leading into the school yard, and then I saw it. The playground. The primary colors of the swing set, the monkey bars, the slides, and the balance beam all gleamed in the moonlight. It was a snapshot of a realized dream. His dream. My middle daughter, Giada, was swinging—higher, back and forth, higher and higher. All was quiet except for my heart and hers singing, for the sound of the chains of that swing.

How many nights had we laid awake in that bedroom dreaming? He just couldn't stop talking about that playground. He wanted to build this for the kids at the school and in the orphanage to jump and play and work out. How he longed for these children, who were marked by poverty and adversity, to run free, to taste the joy he had known as a boy. His own life had been marked by hardship, growing up without a dad, chasing dreams. How many mornings did I find him with his journal making plans and lists of ways we could raise money to build that playground in Haiti? So many times I had believed it was just a pipe dream. So many times I questioned if it was money well-spent. To see it now, I was sure. I was positive in the depths of my soul this playground was an example of His Glory. You see, it started as a little thread—a seed of a dream one man had in his heart—but God watered the seed and so many came along side to cultivate and watch it grow.

I thought about the friends who gathered their talents and their resources in the United States to chase this dream with us. I thought about the friends who ran in a half marathon raising money for that playground. I thought about the friend who made and sold jars of caramel sauce, another who served up Mexican dinners, another who cooked up her special salsa, another who organized a walk-a-thon at a local park, another who used her gift of photography to raise funds. I thought about the glory they experienced in dreaming and serving the Haitians from the other side of the continent. I thought about the friends who researched the playground equipment with Ericlee, who sacrificed time and made the trip down to Haiti to build it. I thought about relationships with Haitian young men that were forged with those American friends. They labored together. They built that playground side by side. Their hearts were joined in the work, in the sweat, in the laughter, and even in the tears.

In that moment, I looked out across the school yard and I saw my own girls lit up with pure joy as they played. They, too, were tasting glory. They were a part of the dream come alive, a legacy continuing. And then I saw the children from the Bridge Christian Children's Home orphanage walking toward me. A few ran, embracing me. The rest stood in line. They were quiet, hugging me and speaking only with their dark eyes. They wanted to know if I was ok. They wanted to know if I was still standing after losing so much.

And I believe they experienced the glory in that moment too. It was a sacred moment. A moment to be savored. Tears pooled in my eyes. These were not tears of sadness. These were tears of joy, gratitude, hope. The kids showed me every facet of the playground. They laughed and balanced and swung. They blessed me with the vision of His glory right there. They showed me how God could bring beauty from ashes.

For the last nine weeks, we have been learning about glory together. We have been climbing and looking and listening. We have been chasing. This may feel like the end of the journey but really it's only the beginning. My prayer is that these weeks have formed in you a habit, a new frame. My hope is that glory chasing is not just an assignment to be completed over a few months, but rather a way of living, and a way of dying. All for His Glory.

GLORY CHASERS

Songs for worship & inspiration this week:

"Your Glory Endures Forever" by Charlie Hall
"Grace So Glorious" by Elevation Worship
"Into the Glorious" by Christy Nockels
"Glory Come Down" by Derek Johnson
"Overwhelmed" by Big Daddy Weave

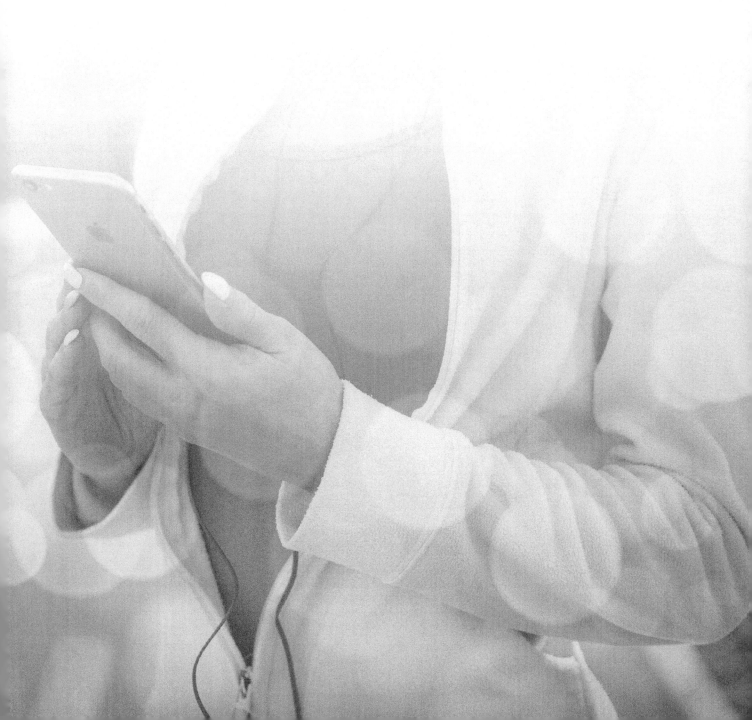

Notes

Glimpses of Glory this Week

Dear Leader Friends,

I just want to thank you for joining me on this adventure of chasing God's glory. As a facilitator of this Bible study, you have a special opportunity to encourage and lead others into a deeper understanding and relationship with Jesus Christ.

Some of the activities in this study may challenge the friends in your group. They might have to step out of their comfort zones to draw a picture or journal a reflection. I hope you will model this for them. I encourage you to take the first step. I know the temptation is to skip over questions or activities that feel different. I hope you will resist that temptation and jump in with both feet. My desire is that anyone who opens these pages will learn to become a Glory Chaser and see glimpses of God's glory all around them.

I am praying over each one of you as you begin this journey. You are a gift to me because you are taking this Glory Chasers study and multiplying the message to new friends in new places. This is how we partner together in the Gospel.

For His Glory,
Dorina

P.S. I would love to hear your experiences with this study. Send me a message at www.DorinaGilmore.com

LEADER GUIDE

WEEK ONE—INTRODUCTION

A creative giveaway:
You might consider bringing a pair of shoelaces for members of your small group or to add to the centerpiece as a tangible way to invite them into this experience. The shoelaces symbolize the invitation to lace up our shoes and get ready to chase His glory in the next 10 weeks.

Take time to process:
Was there something from the worship or teaching time that pricked your heart or resonated with you today?

Take time to discuss:
1. What do I already know about glory? What images (secular or sacred) does this word stir up for me?
2. What do I want to invest in this experience?
3. What do I want to gain from this experience?
4. What is something broken in me where I long to see His glory?
5. What else am I chasing right now in my life that distracts me from seeing His glory?

Take time to pray:
- Pray specifically over the things shared that serve as distractions for the women in your group. *Pray for fresh eyes to see God and His glory during this season.
- Pray for each woman to experience God in a personal way.

Take time to steep in this scripture:
Jesus said to her, "Did I not tell you that if you believed you would see the GLORY of God?" —John 11:40 (ESV)

WEEK TWO—CREATION

A creative giveaway:
You might consider bringing watercolor paint sets, a box of crayons or colored pencils for the members of your small group to invite them into this experience or to use in your centerpiece. This is meant to inspire them this week that we are all God's creation and created to create.

Take time to process:
Was there something from the worship or teaching time that pricked your heart or resonated with you today?

Take time to discuss:
1. What does it mean to you that you are created in God's image?
2. In Genesis 2:19-20, God gives Adam the creative work of naming all the living creatures. Think about your own name or the names of your children. What is significant about these names? How is naming something an act of creation?
3. What are some of the ways you experienced God's glory through Creation this week?
4. As you read Psalm 8 and Psalm 29 for day four, what are some of the things you noticed and learned about glory?
5. Read Ephesians 2:10 aloud as a group in 3 different Bible versions. (Examples: NIV, ESV and The Message or others). What if we decided to believe our purpose in this world really is to reflect the glory of God? What would that look like in your own context today?

Take time to pray:
- Pray for more opportunities to experience God's glory through Creation
- Pray for eyes to see God's glory in your everyday rhythms.
- Pray for courage to be creative in new ways that reflect His glory.

Take time to steep in this scripture:
The heavens declare the glory of God; the sky above proclaims his handiwork. —Psalm 19:1 (ESV)

WEEK THREE—PRESENCE

A creative giveaway:
You might consider bringing votive candles for your small group to invite them into this experience or to use as your centerpiece this week. The candle is a reminder of God's light within us and the presence of the Holy Spirit with us each day.

Take time to process:
Was there something from the worship or teaching time that pricked your heart or resonated with you today?

Take time to discuss:
1. What did you learn about God's glory and presence in reading through the various passages in Exodus?
2. What is unique about the way Elijah experiences God's presence? Have you ever had an unexpected encounter with God?
3. As you read through Luke 2, how did you see Mary entering into the presence of God?
4. As we contemplate God's name Emmanuel, meaning "God with us," which of the verses you read this week was most encouraging?
5. What are some of the ways the Holy Spirit has been present with you?

Take time to pray:
- Pray for God to give you a greater awareness of His presence this week.
- Pray to see His Glory through His Presence and the people He has put in your life to encourage you.
- Pray for the Holy Spirit to give you discernment and peace in your present decisions.

Take time to steep in this scripture:
Then Moses said, "Now show me your glory." —Exodus 33:18 (NIV)

WEEK FOUR—WORSHIP

A creative giveaway:
You might consider bringing dish soap and a cloth for your small group to invite them into this experience or to use in your centerpiece this week. This should serve as a reminder that we can worship in a variety of ways even when we are doing mundane tasks like washing dishes.

Take time to process:
1. Was there something from the worship or teaching time that pricked your heart or resonated with you today?
2. Take time to discuss:
3. What song did you choose to focus on this week and why?
4. In Luke 2:1-20, how did the angels set the tone for Worship of Christ the King?
5. What does Psalm 96 say to you about Worship?
6. What do you think Jesus meant in the story of the Samaritan woman at the well when he talked about worshipping in "spirit and truth"?
7. What are some examples of unexpected ways you learned worship this week?

Take time to pray:
- Pray for God to expand your view of Worship in the weeks to come.
- Pray for reminders to praise Him even through the storms of life.
- Pray for God to help you make worship a lifestyle.

Take time to steep in this scripture:
Sing to the LORD, bless his name; tell of his salvation from day to day. Declare his glory among the nations, his marvelous works among all the peoples! —Psalm 96:2-3

WEEK FIVE—FAME

A creative giveaway:
You might consider bringing a mirror for your small group to invite them into this experience. You could use the mirror as a centerpiece or give out small mirrors as a reminder for the ladies that our identity lies in Christ. When we look in the mirror, we need to view ourselves as He sees us and reflect His glory to those around us.

Take time to process:
Was there something from the worship or teaching time that pricked your heart or resonated with you today?

Take time to discuss:
1. How did God use Joseph to bless the surrounding countries and introduce Himself?
2. Has God ever given you favor or privilege in an unexpected way that presented an avenue to bring Him glory?
3. What did you learn about God's glory and the nations through reading Isaiah 60?
4. What are some reflections you had about the question: Does my life cause people to praise God or me?
5. How does Paul adapt the gospel message for his audience in Acts 17:24-31?

Take time to pray:
- Pray for God to show you the ways you are seeking to glorify yourself instead of Him.
- Pray for eyes to see God in your story—the good chapters and the challenging chapters.
- Pray for ways to creatively share His glory story with your circles of influence.

Take time to steep in this scripture:
I have appointed you for the very purpose of displaying my power in you, and to spread my fame throughout the whole earth. —Romans 9:17 (NLT)

WEEK SIX—SUFFERING

A creative giveaway:
You might consider bringing a small cross for your small group to invite them into this experience. You could use the cross as a centerpiece. The cross is a reminder of the suffering Jesus endured and how we might join Him in suffering for His glory.

Take time to process:
Was there something from the worship or teaching time that pricked your heart or resonated with you today?

Take time to discuss:
1. What kind of suffering did Hagar endure? Can you relate to her story inany way?
2. What was Job's immediate response to the tragedy described in Job 1:13-22?
3. Have you seen God take suffering and make things new for you or someone you know?
4. What nuances or differences did you notice in the three descriptions of the scene at the Garden of Gethsemane?
5. How can you share His Glory with people suffering around you?

Take time to pray:
- Pray for strength to respond with trust when life's circumstances prove difficult.
- Pray for endurance for the everyday afflictions and opportunities to give Him glory.
- Pray for your heart to be in tune to those suffering around you.

Take time to steep in this scripture:
Dear Friends, do not be surprised at the fiery ordeal that has come on you to test you, as though something strange were happening to you. But rejoice inasmuch as you participate in the sufferings of Christ, so that you may be overjoyed when his glory is revealed. —1 Peter 4:12-13 (NIV)

WEEK SEVEN—COMMUNITY

A creative giveaway:
You might consider bringing Legos for your small group to invite them into this experience. You may use these as a centerpiece. The Legos represent our connectedness in community. We can share our resources, build on each other's gifts, and create together for His glory.

Take time to process:
Was there something from the worship or teaching time that pricked your heart or resonated with you today?

Take time to discuss:
1. What did you learn from Acts 2:41-47 about Community?
2. Share your stories about Community.
3. Do you have someone in your life who sharpens you?
4. Describe how some of the pairs mentioned in your Day Four homework depended on each other and made each other better.

Take time to pray:
- Pray for a friend who can sharpen you in your spiritual life and you can sharpen in return.
- Pray for a margin in your schedule to be able to invest in your Community.
- Pray for ways to be Emmanuel to people who might not have strong Community support.

Take time to steep in this scripture:
Let us think of ways to motivate one another to acts of love and good works. And let us not neglect our meeting together, as some people do, but encourage one another, especially now that the day of his return is drawing near. —Hebrews 10:24-25 (NLT)

WEEK EIGHT—JUSTICE

A creative giveaway:
You might consider bringing a red rose or a rose plant for each person in your small group or to use as a centerpiece to invite them into this experience. The rose is the symbol of something that is both difficult and beautiful. The thorns on a rose are used for its protection, painful to the touch, a reminder that justice work is difficult but it is about protecting the oppressed because that's what Jesus did. The red petals are a reminder that beauty can come from ashes. Biblical justice is also a beautiful way we participate in God's glory.

Take time to process:
Was there something from the worship or teaching time that pricked your heart or resonated with you today?

Take time to discuss:
1. After studying this week, how would you define justice?
2. How is justice part of God's heart and the bigger glory story?
3. How can you apply Micah 6:8 to your own context today?
4. Explain what you learned about the Kinsman-Redeemer role in the book of Ruth. How does Boaz participate in justice work that redeems Ruth & Naomi?
5. What is one injustice in our world today that moves you?

Take time to pray:
- Pray for a new understanding of our call to Biblical justice work.
- Pray for the injustices you now see in our world.
- Pray for courage to step up and step into learning more about justice and how you can participate for His glory.

Take time to steep in this scripture:
He has told you, O man, what is good; and what does the LORD require of you but to do justice, and to love kindness, and to walk humbly with your God? —Micah 6:8 (ESV)

WEEK NINE—HEAVEN

A creative giveaway:
You might consider bringing small squares of tulle for your small group or decorating a centerpiece using a wedding veil to invite them into this experience. The tulle is to represent a veil worn by the bride of Christ. We look to Glory and the Grand wedding we will one day experience with the Bridegroom. The church is also often regarded as the Bride of Christ.

Take time to process:
Was there something from the worship or teaching time that pricked your heart or resonated with you today?

Take time to discuss:
1. According to Colossians 3:1-4, how do we share in Christ's glory?
2. What was most striking from the passages you explored about Heaven in Day Two?
3. How do you imagine Heaven?
4. What did you learn about the new earth and new jerusalem?
5. How do the new heaven and new earth reflect the ultimate glory?

Take time to pray:
- Pray against fear of death.
- Pray for a new excitement about the "things above" and what God has in store for us in Heaven.
- Pray for opportunities to share with loved ones and others about the hope we have in Heaven.

Take time to steep in this scripture:
Set your minds on things that are above, not on things that are on earth. For you have died, and your life is hidden with Christ in God. When Christ who is your life appears, then you also will appear with him in glory.
—Colossians 3:2-4 (ESV)

WEEK TEN—CLOSING THOUGHTS— A CELEBRATION OF HIS GLORY

A creative giveaway:

Today we are going to celebrate at the table together. We want to encourage everyone to bring a favorite dish with a recipe. This time is to represent and look toward the Grand Wedding Feast we will enjoy together in Glory one day. Recipes represent families and stories. Have members share about their recipes and why this is a favorite for them or their family.

Take time to process:

Was there something from the worship or teaching time that pricked your heart or resonated with you today?

Take time to discuss:

1. How do you imagine the Wedding Feast in Glory?
2. Go back through your list of "Glimpses of His Glory" and share a few with your small group?
3. How have these 10 weeks changed your perspective or impacted you?
4. How will you plan to chase His glory in the future?

Take time to pray:

- Pray over each person in your group and their heart moving forward.
- Pray for ways to share His Glory with those around you.

Take time to steep in this scripture:

The Word became flesh and moved into the neighborhood. We saw the glory with our own eyes, the one-of-a-kind glory, like Father, like Son, Generous inside and out, true from start to finish. —John 1:14 (MSG)

Closing:

Join hands. Sing a closing worship song together. Choose one from the Spotify playlist or a familiar hymn or chorus.

Suggestion:

"In My Life, Lord, Be Glorified"

END NOTES

WEEK TWO: CREATION

1. Ann Voskamp, *One Thousand Gifts*. (Grand Rapids: Zondervan, 2010), 110.
2. Emily P. Freeman, *A Million Little Ways*. (Grand Rapids, Revell, 2013), 22.
3. Hank Fortener, "The Artisan Soul: Prelude" (sermon, Mosaic Church, February 23, 2014).
4. Erwin McManus, *The Artisan Soul*. (New York: HarperOne, 2015), 23.
5. Emily P. Freeman, *A Million Little Ways*. (Grand Rapids: Revell, 2013), 188.

WEEK THREE: PRESENCE

6. Hillsong United. "Oceans (Where Feet May Fail)" Zion Acoustic Sessions. 2014.
7. "Glory" The Free Dictionary, accessed: August 17, 2016. http://www.thefreedictionary.com/glory

WEEK FIVE: FAME

8. John Piper. "God Created Us for His Glory," Desiring God, July 27, 1980.
9. Chris Tomlin. "Famous One" Passion: Our Love is Loud. 2002.
10. Caryn Rivadeneira, *Known and Loved*. (Grand Rapids, Revell, 2013), 44.
11. Study note on Acts 17:22-31. *The Study Bible for Women: Holman Christian Standard Bible* (Nashville: Holman Christian Bible Publishers, 2014), 1434.

WEEK SIX: SUFFERING

12. Charles Spurgeon. "Why We Can Rejoice In Suffering." Desiring God. October 23, 1994. http://www.desiringgod.org/messages/why-we-can-rejoice-in-suffering
13. Shane and Shane. "Though You Slay Me" Bring Your Nothing. 2013.

14. John Piper with 7 other authors. *Feed My Sheep*. (Sanford, Reformation Trust Publishing, 2008), 258.
15. "Passion" Online Etymology Dictionary, accessed: February 29, 2016. http://www.etymonline.com/ index.php?term=passion.
16. Ann Voskamp. *The Greatest Gift: Unwrapping the Full Love Story of Christmas*. (Tyndale House Publishers, 2013), 79.

WEEK SEVEN: COMMUNITY

17. Emily P. Freeman. *A Million Little Ways*. (Grand & Revell, 2013), 105.
18. "Koinonia" Strong's on Bible Hub, accessed: February 29, 2016. http://biblehub.com/greek/2842.htm.
19. Annie Downs. *Let's All Be Brave*. (Grand Rapids: Zondervan, 2014), 74.

WEEK EIGHT: JUSTICE

20. Dictionary.com, "justice." Accessed August 18, 2017, http://www.dictionary.com/browse/justice?s=t
21. Julie Clawson *Everyday Justice: The Global Impact of Our Daily Choices*. (Intervarsity Press Books, 2009), 20.
22. Mitchel Lee, "Brave Faith: Justice and the Mission of God" (sermon, Grace Community Church, October 19, 2014).
23. Ken Wytsma. *Pursuing Justice*. 2013. (Nashville: Thomas Nelson).
24. Study note on James 1:27. The Study Bible for Women: Holman Christian Standard Bible (Nashville: Holman Christian Bible Publishers, 2014), 1588.
25. R. York Moore. *Making All Things New: God's Dream for Global Justice*. (Downer's Grove: IVP Books, 2012), 124.
26. Ray C. Stedman, commentary. *Highlights of Old Testament History: Wisdom & Prophecy. Joy of Living Series*. http://joyofliving.org/product/highlights-of-the-old-testament-wisdom-prophecy-adult-study-english/,48.
27. Ken Wytsma. *Pursuing Justice*. 2013. (Nashville: Thomas Nelson), 19.

WEEK NINE: HEAVEN

28. Chris Rice. "Untitled Hymn (Come to Jesus)" Short Term Memories. 2004.
29. Randy Alcorn. *Heaven*. (Grand Rapids: Tyndale, 2004), Introduction xix.
30. Randy Alcorn. *Heaven*. (Grand Rapids: Tyndale, 2004), 471.
31. Mercy Me. "I Can Only Imagine" Almost There. 2001.

ACKNOWLEDGEMENTS

I started writing *Glory Chasers* in early 2015, just months after my husband Ericlee graduated to Glory. I knew from the moment we received his diagnosis that he had stage four melanoma cancer that God intended to use our story for His glory. Of course, I had no idea where our story was headed or what the outcome might be. This is not just my story; It's our story.

To Ericlee Gilmore, my late husband, who infused me with courage and faith beyond what I believed I had on my own. You were my running partner and coach, constantly encouraging, challenging and loving me. You beat me to the finish line, but I will meet you in Glory one day.

To my three daughters, Meilani, Giada and Zayla, who cheered me on every step of the way. Your tireless love and hugs for your imperfect mama are a true gift to me. Thank you for your grace when I was writing in every crack of time I could find.

To my husband Shawn Young, who championed this project from start to finish. You offered a keen editing eye, a sound business mind and a sacrificial love that I needed to chase this project to completion. Thank you for continuing to dream and pray with me.

To my parents Doug and Maria Lazo, who have cultivated my gift of writing since I was in grade school. Thanks, Mom, for always being an honest editor and a relentless cheerleader. To my mother-in-law Christene, who gave her time to help watch my kids so I could write.

To Mitchel Lee, who first introduced me to the idea of being a "glory chaser." Thank you for continuing to inspire and challenge me with your sermons!

To the first Glory Experience group, my heart friends, Stacie Benedict, Cori Schmidt, Heather Fenton, Allison Vasquez, Brandy Freeland, Jennifer Schultz, Julie Tullis, Susan Holman, and Marcy Pusey, who received the "down draft" of this project with such grace. Thank you for journeying with me through grief and glory.

To my editing friends, Beth Nicoletto, Sybil Kolbert, and Pastor Chris Calvert, who offered up gentle suggestions and abundant praise for this project. I am forever grateful for your time and investment.

To my friends at The Bridge Fresno women's Bible study groups, especially Kathy Moore, Marie Kenyon and all the group leaders, who jumped into this race with me wholeheartedly and opened the doors for me to teach.

To the others in my community, including Troy Vasquez, Michael Fenton, Forest Benedict, Cindy Timberlake Van Heyst, Jennifer Vander Meulen, Brenda Round, Whitney Bunker, Melissa Danisi and many others who offered creative advice, inspiration and support for this project. You were like my aid station, offering that cool drink of water on the journey.

To my Go Mama Workout and runner friends, my Chai sisters, my Hope*Writer friends and the women of The Haitian Bead Project, who have been my community of support. Thank you for running this race with me and sharing your glimpses of glory along the trail. Your glory stories have helped me keep going. And all this, for His glory and our good.

Made in the USA
Coppell, TX
02 April 2024

30814171R00103